The First Five Years

Dr Hugh Jolly

answers questions from parents

Winston Press

Managing Editor Susan Pinkus
Production Manager David Alexander
Photographic Coordination Anna Campen,
                                     Juliet Sansom
Administration Aline Davis, Sonia White

DR. HUGH JOLLY is one of the world's most eminent
pediatricians whose excellent advice and guidance over the
years has helped not only his own patients but also –
through his highly regarded books published
internationally – countless other parents and children.

By the same author:

Sexual Precocity
Diseases of Children
Common Sense about Babies and Children
Book of Child Care
More Commonsense about Babies and Children

Photography by Anthea Sieveking

Winston Press, Inc.
430 Oak Grove
Minneapolis, Minnesota 55403

© 1984 Pagoda Books, 30 Museum Street,
London WC1A 1LH

Publisher's Note
The advice contained in **THE FIRST FIVE YEARS** cannot embrace
all circumstances, nor is it intended as a substitute for individual
consultation with a doctor. Serious problems will, of course, require
urgent and sometimes prompt medical care.

ISBN 0-86683-848-1
Library of Congress Catalog Card Number: 84-50004

Origination by East Anglian Engraving Co. Ltd.
Typeset by D.P. Press Limited, Sevenoaks, Kent
Printed in Great Britain by Cambus Litho, East Kilbride, Scotland

The First Five Years

Dr Hugh Jolly

answers questions from parents

Contents

Introduction

This is the age of the phone-in so we have all become accustomed, while searching the air waves for an interesting program, to tune in on an intimate conversation between a listener at home and a radio presenter in the studio. The popularity of such programs suggested that a similar fomula might be successful in book form, hence the birth of this book.

Parents are today more avid than ever for information on how to achieve the best for their children, especially in terms of discipline and development. It is this which has led to the numerous books, articles and radio and TV programs on the subject. It is a salutary thought, too, that a parent will ask a stranger a personal question on radio, forgetting the millions who are also listening. I sometimes fear that doctors have created this state of affairs by appearing to be too 'busy' during office visits or by making a parent feel that his or her problem is too trivial. In my Utopia, the patient or parent would be handled by the doctor in such a way that he or she feels the doctor has no other patient that day.

In creating the book, authenticity was essential. This was achieved by the publishers, who questioned many hundreds of parents for the most frequent problems they would like answered to help them in bringing up their young children. The questions have been grouped into appropriate sections, and I have answered them personally, in the intimate manner which is essential to a phone-in. Each answer is intended to be complete on its own, so some parents may choose to look up those questions that are of concern to them at a particular time, rather than reading the book straight through from cover to cover. For further information, I hope the reader will refer to my BOOK OF CHILD CARE.

In reading this book, parents should soon become aware that they are not alone in many of their anxieties. I hope, too, that the answers to certain very common areas of parental concern will lead to family discussions on child care, to the benefit of the children.

HUGH JOLLY

The Newborn

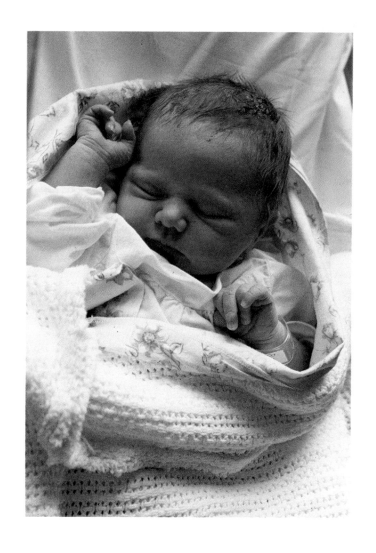

Q How should we pick up our newborn baby and put him down? We still feel awkward when doing so, even after two weeks, and are terrified we might drop him.

I am not surprised that you still feel awkward at two weeks if you have not had much experience with babies beforehand. Having watched hundreds of mothers and fathers handling their very young babies, I am aware how alarming this can be. So please don't feel ashamed of yourselves and imagine that you will never get confidence.

It helps enormously if you have a sympathetic and sensitive nurse or doctor to show you the best way to hold and to put down your baby. The first essential is to feel comfortable yourself so that you aren't afraid of losing your balance. Be sure to hold him securely in both arms and be particularly careful to support his head, which otherwise will wobble about. He cannot support it himself yet. His head should be lying in the crook of one of your arms when you carry him.

As you put him down, support his head with the other hand until his bottom touches the mattress. Then slowly lower his head until it, too, is on the mattress.

I would like all school children to get experience in holding babies. It should be part of a course in education for parenthood. Those who come from a large family and have younger brothers and sisters are quite remarkably competent.

It is always interesting watching a group of new nurses caring for young babies. Those with previous experience are totally at ease, while others handle the babies as though they fear they will break if they do something wrong. In fact, I am always amazed how much a baby will tolerate by way of rough handling—not that I recommend it.

Once you feel competent, you will enjoy showing other parents and children how to hold and to put down a baby. This will also increase your own confidence.

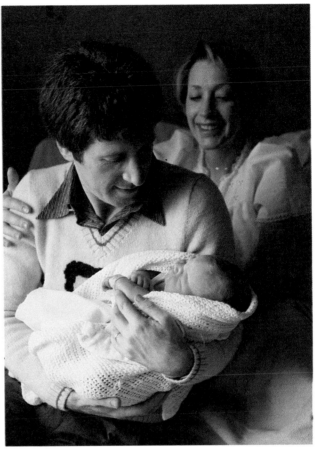

The newborn probably looks very fragile; but babies are actually far hardier than they seem, and confidence in handling an infant will soon be gained.

Q Why has our newborn developed jaundice?

Less oxygen is available to the fetus *in utero*, compared with someone living in the normal atmosphere. Nature compensates for this by providing the fetus with extra blood and thereby extra capacity for carrying oxygen. After birth, this extra blood is no longer required, so it is broken down in the liver, producing a yellow pigment called *bilirubin*.

If the liver is functioning well, it can prevent any accumulation of bilirubin, but in many babies, especially those born prematurely, the liver—like a factory working at half-strength—cannot keep pace. Consequently, there is an accumulation of bilirubin, which makes the baby look yellow. He is not ill, though he may be extra sleepy, and the accumulation is insufficient to harm the brain.

All the other causes of jaundice in the newborn are much rarer but more serious. A common cause in days gone by was a clash between the mother's blood and that of her baby due to the Rhesus (Rh) blood group. This only occurs if the mother is Rh negative, the father Rh positive, and the baby Rh positive. Some of the baby's cells cross the placenta during birth, causing the mother to form Rhesus antibodies that would damage the red blood cells in her next Rhesus-positive fetus. This is now prevented by giving her an injection immediately after birth to destroy the baby's red cells that have crossed into her blood.

A clash can also occur involving the other blood groups A, B, and O, but the jaundice is mild and seldom harmful.

Black babies, Chinese babies, and those from Mediterranean countries are liable to be born without an enzyme that is required for the normal strength of red blood cells. Consequently, their red blood cells are destroyed more rapidly than normal ones, causing jaundice. This occurs particularly after eating certain foods so that those affected with this problem are given a list of foods and medicines that they must avoid.

Infection is the most serious cause of jaundice, but doctors are so aware of this that if a baby loses his appetite, they act immediately to check whether infection is present.

Treatment of the jaundiced baby depends in part on the cause. For example, a baby whose jaundice is due to infection will be given antibiotics. Additionally, in all jaundiced babies, the level must not be allowed to rise so high that the brain is at risk of damage. This is prevented by ensuring an adequate intake of fluid by mouth, tube-feeding, if necessary, and by giving light treatment. This is termed *phototherapy*, the baby being placed in a special cradle or incubator and exposed to a white light until the jaundice drops to a safe level. Treatment to change the baby's blood (exchange transfusion) is seldom required today. Babies with only mild jaundice will be allowed home if adequate supervision can be maintained.

Q What exactly is the Guthrie Test?

The Guthrie Test, named after its discoverer, is used to exclude a disease called phenylketonuria or PKU. The test has to be carried out on the sixth day of life by the hospital nurse or by the doctor if you have left the hospital. It involves pricking the baby's heel to obtain a drop of blood. This is allowed to soak into a small piece of filter paper that acts like blotting paper. It is then sent to a special laboratory.

You would be told if the test was positive in your baby, but this is very rare. The importance of the test is that, when PKU is diagnosed early in life, the severe mental handicap it causes can be prevented by putting the child on a special diet so that the chemical products produced by the body's abnormal chemistry are prevented from forming.

Q My baby was born three days ago and my breasts have suddenly become red and swollen from engorgement. What can I do about this? Why has this happened?

The system of lactation operates on a basis that the breasts do not make milk until the baby is born. This is related to changes in hormone levels and it is not usual for the breasts to fill up until about the third day. Prior to that, a deeper yellow milk in small quantities is secreted by the breasts. This is *colostrum*. It is very good for the baby, particularly in reducing the risk of some infections.

The ideal management of engorgement is to put the baby to the breast. Through feeding, the breasts become less swollen. But this may not be possible either because the breasts are too engorged for milk to flow, or because the baby's sucking causes pain. In that case, milk can be less painfully removed by using an electric or hand pump, in addition to local and general measures to reduce the pain. Local measures comprise hot towels and extra support applied to the breast. General measures comprise pain relievers, which the obstetrician will prescribe. Estrogen tablets may also be prescribed by the doctor.

Q My baby is four days old and my nipples are sore. Is there anything I can do to relieve the pain?

Sore nipples are very common and there are lots of different reasons for the problem. I am sure that some first-time mothers, for very human reasons, are so frightened of breastfeeding that the normal nip felt as the baby latches on makes them very worried. Almost all mothers tell me that the baby pinches the nipple when he first attaches to the breast, but this passes very rapidly. As you get used to breastfeeding, you will find the discomfort no longer occurs.

Formerly, one of the reasons for sore nipples was the old system of feeding by the clock, so that many babies were left to get very hungry instead of being fed as soon as they wanted. Now that the approach is one of demand-feeding (or, as I prefer to call it, ask-feeding) the baby sucks less vigorously and the nip is less sharp.

You may well have read that leaving the baby on the breast causes sore nipples—a point I was taught as a medical student. I am quite clear that this is incorrect, and that the baby who makes the nipple sore by vigorous sucking is the one who is being fed by the clock and also restricted to ten minutes on each side, another piece of old-fashioned nonsense. A baby soon senses that his time on the breast is going to be restricted, so it is almost as though he is going faster if time is nearly up. "Ask-feeding" means that the baby is fed whenever he wants. He asks by crying, and the more quickly his mother responds to his request, the less vigorously he is likely to suck. Because there is no limitation on time, the baby sucks more gently and may take a number of rests, so that the chance of sore nipples is very much less.

I am conscious that some mothers complain of sore nipples when really they are indicating that they do not want to breastfeed, although they are unable to say so directly or may not even be aware of the fact. It is usually possible for a doctor who is sensitive to the problems of mothers to detect this. The very way a mother describes her feelings about breastfeeding often gives the problem away. Moreover, when you only touch the nipple, the mother screws her face up. Such mothers need help to understand the mechanism of why they feel sore.

If a mother complains of sore nipples and examination shows these to be red and perhaps even to have a crack, the nipple needs to be protected during feedings. This can be achieved by the use of a nipple shield, which is either a rubber cap, fitting over the nipple, or an ordinary type of teat attached to a plastic base that fits over the nipple. The baby is able to draw the milk through the artificial teat by sucking vigorously.

There is one trick that you can try out before using a nipple shield. The aim is to get the baby to compress a different part of the nipple. The baby is placed in the "twin position" so that his body is under the armpit with his legs pointing backwards. This causes the nipple to be compressed at right angles to the line of normal compression, and many mothers find that they lose the pain altogether.

If all these measures fail, there is no alternative but to rest the nipple completely by stopping the baby from feeding from the breast. The milk is expressed by hand or by a pump. I no longer recommend painting the crack with any special preparation. Stopping feeding allows it to heal very rapidly. The only problem is that the crack may recur. To reduce this chance, it is wise to use a shield on the first few occasions when feeding is resumed.

In the old days, pre-natal clinics used to advise scrubbing the nipples. I am glad to say that this extraordinary practice has disappeared.

Q **Could smoking during the period for which I am breastfeeding harm our baby in any way? Might alcohol get through to the baby in the milk?**

Obviously, you are aware that smoking in pregnancy can have the effect of making a baby smaller than he might otherwise have been. Smoking during the period you are breastfeeding could also harm him,

but for a different reason. There is definite evidence that babies brought up in homes where smoking occurs are more liable to chest infections in the early months of life. I must therefore advise you not to smoke.

I only hope, since smoking has so many harmful effects to adults and children that, once you have stopped it for the period you are breastfeeding, you will not take it up again. If your husband smokes, you must try to persuade him to stop, too.

The alcohol you drink is likely to come through in the breast milk in small quantities, but I have never heard of a baby being harmed from the direct effect of the alcohol. The danger is in pregnancy, as I expect you know, because alcohol affects the baby so that he does not grow as rapidly as he should and is also liable to develop abnormalities, particularly of the limbs.

Q **I have been breastfeeding our baby for four months. How· will I know when he is ready to be weaned?**

The simple answer is that he will no longer be satisfied with a diet of milk only when he is ready to be weaned. It will be clear to you that he is still hungry after he has taken a full breast or a bottle feeding.

As you are breastfeeding, you will be able to increase the amount of milk he gets by keeping him on the breast for longer. For as long as he sucks, the breast will go on producing milk. The concept that a baby can empty the breasts is incorrect. Normally, I have always been able to express milk from a mother's breasts when her baby has finished feeding. This means that you can continue to feed by breast alone for as long as it suits you both. It is recommended that you should breastfeed exclusively for the first six months, but if you wish, you can give nothing but breast milk for the whole of the first year.

Weaning will be easier if you have started solids by between six and twelve months, because your baby will already be used both to new tastes and to new ways of eating. But many mothers continue with some breast feedings, particularly early morning and last thing at night, until well into the second year. Both babies and mothers are commonly loathe to give up the breast, so that weaning is likely to be a gradual process for you, for reasons of sheer comfort and pleasure.

If you had been bottle-feeding, it would not be a good idea to increase the recommended amount of milk. Cows' milk is much more fattening than breast milk and this excess fat would be harmful to the baby. For this reason, artificially fed babies are usually started on solids when they are

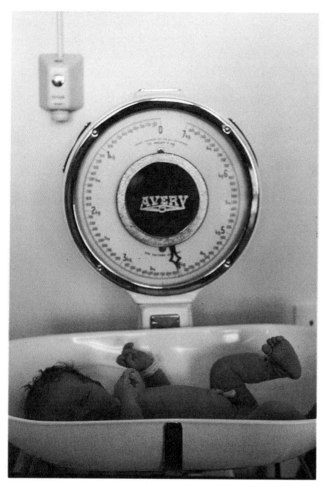

three to four months old.

Perhaps the most important point to emphasize is to ensure that you do not feel confined to rules about how and when to wean. Adopt an experimental approach. Your baby will then get used to changes and you will be more confident.

Q **Our four-day-old seems to have lost weight. Is this anything to worry about? Will he start to gain soon?**

It is normal for a baby to lose a few ounces in the first three or four days of life. This is usually made up by the tenth day and sometimes earlier. A normal full-term baby does not require much food or water in the early days. He will get all he needs from the breast. A supplementary feeding is quite unnecessary for the normal baby.

However, do not hesitate to ask the doctor about this loss of weight because the amount that can safely be lost is variable, depending on the birth weight and the general condition of the baby. As long as the baby is eating normally there

is seldom any cause for concern. Your doctor or pediatrician will decide how often your baby should be weighed.

As all mothers who have breastfed know, the milk does not arrive for the first three days when the breasts suddenly become full. Small quantities of concentrated yellow-colored milk called *colostrum* have been produced before then. This is a high-protein food and nothing more is needed. If the baby was starving, he would cry, but in fact he sleeps most of the time.

In the same way, it is incorrect to give the baby a bottle feeding at this time, but it is difficult to stop nurses and mothers from doing so because the milk is there and, unless well taught, they imagine the baby must be fed.

Q **Is it essential to bottle-feed our baby with warmed milk?**

There is no need to warm the milk given by bottle. Babies in the hospital are often given milk straight from the refrigerator. For years I have done this, wondering if I would find a baby refusing the cold milk but none of them has.

Take care that your infant is not gaining weight too quickly. If you are bottle-feeding, check that the formula is mixed correctly. Breastfed babies are rarely overweight since supply is closely linked to demand. There are certainly many advantages to breastfeeding: but the mother who opts to bottle-feed for whatever reason need not feel her baby is necessarily deprived: for what matters, too, is the loving way in which a baby is fed, as part of the process of bonding.

But this seems to make sense in relation to adults, too. I hate warm milk but love cold milk and I believe this is true for most adults.

I suspect the idea that babies must have warm milk comes from the fact that breast milk is warm. Consequently, mothers naturally feel they ought to give the bottle at the same temperature.

If you use warm milk, keep it warm during the feeding by placing it in a jug of warm water between your baby's short rest periods while feeding. Alternatively, you can use one of the warming covers available on the market. Under no circumstances should you feed your baby reheated milk because germs will have grown in the absence of proper sterilization.

The amount of time you will save by not warming the milk will be enormous. One more trick to make life easier for the busy mother!

Q **Will I be able to breastfeed if I fall ill?**

Whether or not it would be wise to continue breastfeeding will depend on your illness and also on how ill you are feeling. If your illness is highly contagious, then the risk to your baby must come first. But if you have a cold, I suggest you continue to breastfeed because your baby will already be infected, though he may not get the symptoms.

Having said this, I think too many doctors stop mothers from breastfeeding when they would like to continue. If, therefore, there is no risk of harm, to you or to your baby, I suggest you tell your doctor that you wish to continue. It will be good for you to feel that your baby is not losing out by your being ill and you will avoid the misery of being without him. Remember, too, that suddenly stopping breastfeeding is likely to be associated with painful engorgement of the breasts.

If you have to go into the hospital, the nurses in an adult ward may not be used to the techniques of breastfeeding, let alone looking after babies. But I hope they will be sensible enough to call on the children's ward to lend a nurse at times both to help you and to teach them.

Q **We suspect our baby may have thrush. He has white patches inside his cheeks and on his tongue.**

Your description certainly sounds like thrush, especially if it is difficult to scrape off the white patches with the handle of a spoon. This test differentiates thrush from milk sticking to the lining of the cheeks and tongue, since this is easily removed.

Thrush is due to a fungus called *candida albicans* and is common in bottle-fed babies since the utensils used easily become contaminated if not sterilized properly. It is rare in babies who are totally breastfed and are nursed with their mothers since the mother would need to have thrush infection of the breasts, which is uncommon. But of course, if a breastfed baby was placed in a nursery where a baby did have thrush, contamination from staff failing to wash hands after handling the infected baby could allow transfer of the fungus.

It makes feeding painful so that it may be obvious to you that it hurts your baby to suck even though he or she wants to. It may also cause a diaper rash since the thrush fungus is present in the stools.

Most cases respond quickly to the modern forms of treatment available to your doctor such as *nystatin*, an antibiotic. However, it is essential to check why the thrush fungus reached the baby and to go through the sterilizing procedures very carefully if you are bottle-feeding.

Q The doctor says that our newborn baby has a blocked tear duct. What causes this? What can be done about it? Is it likely that he will need an operation? How should it be treated?

The tear duct is the channel that drains the tears from the inside of the eye into the upper part of the nose. Because tears are passed down into the nose, someone who is crying sniffs as well in order to prevent his or her nose running.

Tears are made in a gland that lies in the outer and upper part of the eye, under the eyelid, so that tears naturally pass across the cornea (the clear part of the eye) to drain into the tear duct.

A blocked tear duct is not uncommon and causes the baby to have watering from the eyes. The eyes may not only water but produce a sticky discharge, sometimes as a result of infection—a problem known as a "sticky eye."

The mothers' task with a blocked tear duct is very simple. If the only symptom is excessive watering, she only needs to dry the lower eyelid or cheek from time to time. On the other hand, if the child develops a "sticky eye," the child should be seen by a doctor. In most instances of "sticky eye," the eyeball is not inflamed and the stickiness has developed as a reaction to amniotic fluid and blood that got into the eye during the process of birth. This shows itself within the first three days of life. If this occurs, the mother simply has to clean the eyes with cotton, being sure to start near the nostril and moving outwards.

A "sticky eye" that develops after the age of three or four days is more often due to an infection, and the eyeball may be inflamed. This must, of course, be seen by a doctor who will usually treat the condition with an antibiotic ointment placed just inside the lower eyelid when this is turned out using the forefinger.

The most common reason for blockage of the tear duct is that it has not yet opened to the full, and possibly is blocked with debris that will disappear as soon as it grows to full size. Many children who have a blocked tear duct, which may be in one or in both eyes, have a rather shallow bridge to the nose. In consequence, the space for the tear duct is smaller than normal and so not large enough to allow the flow of tears. As the baby grows, so does the tear duct, with the result that by the time he or she is a year old, the problem of watering from the eye has disappeared. This nose shape is more common in those who are of negro origin, so they more often get a blocked tear duct.

Because the duct opens of its own accord with growth in most instances, the eye specialist does not normally do anything until at least the age of six months. If the eye is still watering then, and very few are, the specialist will probe the eye under a general anesthetic. He uses a very fine probe, since the duct is naturally very small, and gently pushes it through into the nose so as to widen the duct and clear away any debris that is preventing the free flow of tears.

Q One hears such a lot about crib deaths. It must be dreadful for the parents. Is there any known cause? What are the principal factors that come into play?

I can think of no greater tragedy for a family than for them to find that their baby is dead in his crib. The baby is usually about three to six months old and, in the majority of cases, no cause can be found. Sometimes the baby may not have been quite himself the day before because of an infection. It is for this reason that parents are warned always to take their baby to the doctor if he seems at all off-color, and particularly if he has refused a feeding. Even if he has been completely well until the tragedy is discovered, an examination after death may show evidence of an overwhelming infection so that nothing could possibly have been done to save the child.

Many different factors may account for the problem. For example, from experimental evidence with guinea pigs, it seems a guinea pig can become so sensitive to cows' milk that this can kill it. However, present evidence is that whether a human baby is breast- or bottle-fed has no bearing on crib deaths. There was a time when it was felt that breastfeeding was a safeguard, and that the high sodium content of cows' milk was a possible factor. Calves require a milk with a relatively high level of sodium, but human babies can become ill from an excess of it. It is for this reason that some years ago all cows' milk preparations for babies under six months had to have a low sodium content.

One of the most tragic effects of a crib death is the inevitable guilt felt by the parents, particularly if they have been handled insensitively by doctors, nurses, or the police. The only advice one can give to parents is, I repeat, to call the doctor if ever you think your baby is unwell.

There is a constant fear that a baby may smother if a pillow is used, and for this reason it is recommended that babies under the age of twelve months lie on a firm mattress and without a pillow.

Equally as important is the lining of the crib, which should not be plastic, since a baby could move himself so that his nose lay up against the plastic, causing his breathing to be obstructed.

It used to be believed that babies could be smothered by being "overlain" when sleeping in the parents' bed. This is incorrect and many families now practice the "family bed," whereby the baby—like other mammals—sleeps close to his mother. The one important point to make to all parents is that they should never have their baby in bed with them if either of them has taken a sleeping pill or is under the influence of alcohol.

Many mothers are frightened by the way a normal baby may breathe with shallow respirations and appear very pale. The mother in her panic then prods her baby who immediately screams, and she feels stupid. I would like all mothers to know that this is an entirely normal fear, and there can be few mothers who have not experienced such anxieties.

Q **Our baby was born with a harelip. Can we expect that the surgical treatment will be successful? When is it likely to be carried out? Will I be able to stay in hospital with our baby when he has the operation?**

You have used the old term "harelip", although today most people prefer to talk of a "cleft lip". I am glad to know your baby has not got an associated cleft palate, since the treatment will be much simpler. I hope you have been shown photographs of similarly affected babies at birth and after treatment. You will then know how excellent are the results of modern surgery and feel less distressed.

Since your baby does not have a cleft palate as well, feeding will be easier and you are less likely to need any of the methods described on page 19. The operation, undertaken by a plastic surgeon, is likely to be at about three months of age. The baby must be thriving and not anemic. Most surgeons like the baby to have reached ten pounds in weight. Insist that you stay in the hospital with him when he has the operation, whether or not you are breastfeeding. He needs you, and your presence will lessen his crying and speed his recovery. You can certainly expect a successful result and modern surgeons can make the scar invisible. The surgeon will decide when your baby can eat normally. Some like the baby to be tube-fed for a few days so that there is no pull on the newly united lip. Similarly, the surgeon will decide when you can

go home; this is usually about a week after the operation. If the cleft is a large one, he may need to operate in two stages for perfection, especially if the corner of the nose is misshapen. You may have wondered if there is a risk for your future babies having a similar problem. Mostly it occurs in only one child in a family but there is an approximate risk of 1:25 for your future children and a similar risk for his or her children later on.

Q **What causes cradle cap? The doctor has diagnosed this. What treatment is best?**

Cradle cap is caused by dandruff. It makes the scalp look brown because of the layer of dandruff covering it. The condition is very common and is due to excessive greasiness of the scalp as in adults who, because they have more hair, may find they have flakes of dandruff caught in it. Cradle cap is not contagious but sometimes it can cause red scaly inflammation of the adjoining skin. It may also cause cracks in the skin where the top of the ear joins the head.

The area of the scalp most often affected is the part overlying the anterior fontanel, the official name for the gap in the bones on the top of the head and often called "the soft spot". Understandably, mothers are sometimes frightened to wash the scalp thoroughly over the soft spot in case they harm the baby's brain. In fact, a tough membrane totally protects the baby's brain so you can shampoo as hard over the soft spot as you can elsewhere on the baby's head.

All that is needed to get rid of the problem in most babies is regular (daily at first), thorough washing of the scalp with a baby shampoo. It is important to get rid of the crusts when they first appear. Sometimes this needs a solution of one teaspoon of sodium bicarbonate to one pint of water. Alternatively, you can soak the crusts overnight with arachis or olive oil to loosen them and then gently lift them off with a comb.

In severe cases, especially if the surrounding skin is inflamed, you would be wise to ask the advice of your doctor.

Q **How can we prevent our baby getting diaper rash? How is it caused?**

The best way to avoid diaper rash is to change your baby as soon as he is wet or has a bowel action. Leaving him without diapers, when practical, is also a good idea. Breastfeeding babies suffer less from diaper rashes than those

Make sure that your baby's room is at a suitable temperature. Hypothermia – that is, excessive chilling – can be very dangerous for an infant, even a killer: and overheating should be avoided, too. For a newborn baby, the ideal temperature will be about 25° C (75° F), but this can soon be reduced to 20-21° C (68-70° F). If your baby is outside during cold weather, see that he or she is warmly wrapped.

who are bottle-fed.

Make sure you use a pure soap for washing diapers (unless you use disposables); never use a detergent, which causes a rash with some babies. Hang the diapers outside to dry if the weather is fine and the size of your yard allows. Mothers in China circumvent the problem of diaper rash by hanging their laundry on poles that protrude from the window of the flat. They also do without diapers by using suits and underclothes that are slit at the back, leaving no clothes to be soiled when the child squats down because the slit opens automatically when stretched.

The commonest type of diaper rash results from the formation of ammonia in the diaper which burns the skin. This ammonia is formed by the action of germs from the bowel that do no harm to the baby, acting on the urea in the urine so that it gives off ammonia. Ammonia is alkaline, so if the diaper is made acid by a final rinse in vinegar (one ounce of vinegar to one gallon of water) the ammonia does not form. Benzalkonium chloride ointment has the same action in preventing the formation of urea and should be used as well on the baby's bottom as a preventive measure.

Thrush, a fungus that causes white spots in the mouth, also produces diaper rash. It is easily treated once diagnosed, using an antibiotic cream.

Q **Is it safe to put our baby outside in the buggy in chilly weather? Or is it essential he is indoors?**

As long as the child was appropriately clothed, it used to be thought perfectly safe to put your baby outside. In fact, it used to be the standard pattern of child care in those who had yards. The question is whether in fact it is desirable, and why there seems to have been a complete change so that I would suspect that few mothers do this now.

I do not think it is desirable other than for short periods. The old theory was that a child was made more healthy by being "weathered" but no notice was taken of his social needs, in particular his need for company. I find myself appalled to think that babies were just left in a boring buggy to spend a great deal of the day sleeping. This meant that they missed out on so many of the learning opportunities that hopefully

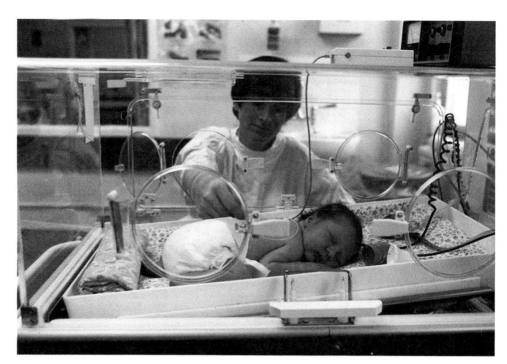

The premature baby, born before the 35th week of pregnancy and weighing less than 2.3 kg (5 pounds), will probably be placed in an incubator, which will recreate the environment of the womb and protect the infant from infection. His system is not yet sufficiently mature to cope alone. Once the baby has caught up in size, however, can breathe normally and does not need to take nourishment by tube, he or she will be allowed home.

parents provide today. If a child is left outside in a buggy he should not only be suitably clothed but also have his interest stimulated. He could watch the movement of leaves, for instance, if placed near a tree.

I would emphasize that activity in the form of play is far more important than sleeping. This means that today's approach, emphasizing activity with a child indoors or outdoors, is preferable to the long periods of sleep in a buggy that was so much the fashion in previous generations.

One final point: if you have a cat, you must protect your baby with a cat net, whether he is indoors or outdoors. Cats particularly enjoy lying in buggies and portacribs, with a special tendency to lie on the baby's head. Remember, too, that cats often stray into yards, so even if you do not have a pet of your own, you will need a cat net.

You will be wise, too, to have your baby fairly near the house so that you are within earshot. Do not leave him or her in an area to which there may be access by a stranger either.

Q **We have noticed that our baby has a swollen navel and are worried about him. What could be wrong? Could it be a hernia of some kind?**

This is almost certainly an umbilical hernia. It comprises a protrusion of intestine so that the umbilicus (navel) sticks out. No treatment is required. As the umbilical scar shrinks, so the protrusion disappears.

In previous times the treatment was to strap the umbilicus, but it was shown that spontaneous cure took longer if this method was used.

Q **How long will it take our premature baby to catch up in size and weight?**

The term "premature baby" though still used loosely requires qualification because there are two types of low birth weight babies with very different causes and problems. A low birth weight baby is defined as one whose birth weight is 5½ pounds or under: and the two groups are those whose low weight results from being born too early—the preterm baby—and those who are underweight because of starvation *in utero*—the "small for dates" baby. Babies may also be born small from a combination of both causes.

The preterm baby is faced with problems resulting from immature organs while the "small for dates" baby is suffering from malnutrition. There are many causes for each; for example, one of the commonest causes for preterm labor is a cervix that is not tightly closed (cervical incompetence). This may be the result of a previous termination of pregnancy. The reason for a baby being "small for dates" commonly lies in poor placental function preventing optimum feeding of the baby. This may be the result of toxemia of pregnancy and high blood pressure. If your baby is in the preterm group, he is much more likely to catch up in weight and size though the chances are reduced if he was very small. The "small for dates" baby has suffered from lack of growth at a crucial time and is much less likely to achieve the size expected than if he had not had this problem.

As a general guide, your baby will continue to catch up in his growth during the first two to three years. After that, he will maintain the average rate of growth for normal babies of that age. Of course, your own height and your husband's will also be a strong influence in determining his rate of growth and his ultimate height.

Q **My husband would like to have our newborn baby in bed with us but friends tell us it is dangerous because of the possibility of overlying. They also say we will make a rod for our back. What should we do?**

Your wish to have your baby in bed with you is perfectly natural; in fact, humans are the only mammals who do not sleep with their young. It is perfectly safe as long as neither you nor your husband have taken a sleeping pill or are under the influence of alcohol.

We once filmed a baby in bed with his parents using a slow-running camera. This enabled us to record a long period of the night and then to view the result at speed. The baby lay between his sleeping parents, and as he moved towards each adult in turn throughout the night, the adult moved away from him as a reflex reaction so that no harm came to the baby.

You will certainly not make a rod for your back, if only because you are meeting your baby's needs in a manner which his age requires. It is those who deny these needs who run into trouble. Of course, if a mother is breastfeeding, she will also find it easier and more convenient.

Q **What exactly is croup? How should it be treated?**

Croup is a term that tends to be used loosely but should be applied only to wheezing resulting from inflammation of the larynx, or vocal cords, in acute laryngitis.

You will notice that your child's breathing has become difficult and is accompanied by a croak. Meanwhile, his cry becomes hoarse. The cause of the symptoms is the narrowing of the larynx from swelling of the vocal cords resulting from inflammation. This is usually mild, though the fear that any difficulty in breathing creates will often make it worse. It is therefore essential that you stay with your child to comfort him.

Because of its danger, the old-fashioned remedy of a steam-kettle has been replaced by a cold water vaporizer. This can be bought for use at home if your child gets repeated attacks. Sitting your child on your knee in the bathroom with the hot tap running to create steam may help if you do not have a vaporizer.

The main question is when to call the doctor and this must be determined by how serious is the child's difficulty in breathing. The noise itself doesn't matter, but if breathing is labored so that the chest is sucked in with each breath, you must contact your doctor. If he is not immediately available, go directly to the hospital emergency department.

Q **Our baby was born with a dislocated hip. Can you explain the treatment that will be given?**

I am sorry to hear that your baby has a dislocated hip but it is a great relief to know that it has been diagnosed immediately because early treatment is essential for a perfect result. Special examination of the hips in all newborn babies is routine so that the trouble is diagnosed within the first day or two of life.

The type of treatment used will depend on the views of the orthopedic surgeon who will be the specialist who looks after your child's hip. The one essential is that the hip should be splinted in such a way as to keep the head of the thigh bone (the femur) in its socket.

Some surgeons use metal splints that are soft enough to be bent to fit each baby. Others use plaster of Paris. Some surgeons prefer a double diaper or a thick pillow between the legs, which acts in the same way.

As the early days pass, the muscles become firmer and stronger so that they ensure that the hip joint remains in the correct position in which it has been held by the various forms of splinting. Treatment lasts a few months until the surgeon is satisfied that there is no risk of the bone coming out of its socket. The results are perfect in almost all cases, whereas in the old days with delayed diagnosis the condition caused a permanent limp.

The cause is laxity or looseness of the bag or capsule that surrounds the hip joint. The condition is present at birth and is sometimes inherited. The baby is not in pain and she tolerates her splint without fuss so that she will be able to go home at the normal time and continue to be supervised as an outpatient.

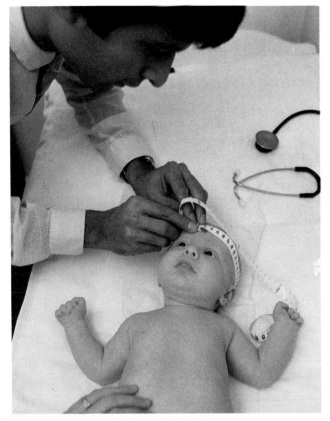

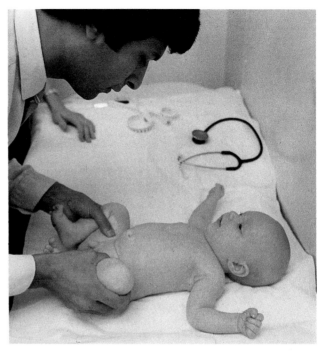

Your baby's early check-ups will include being weighed and *measured, examination for congenital dislocation of the hip,* *reflex reactions and response to sound, among other factors.*

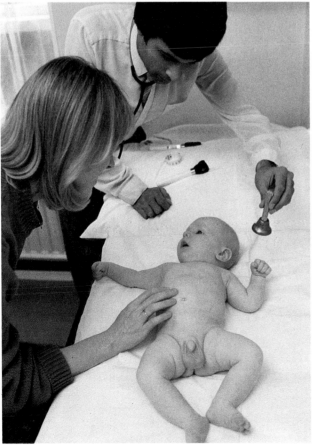

Q **What sort of tests should we expect our baby will be given at his regular checkups at the clinic? How vital is it that he should be advanced in all areas of development?**

The tests applied will be appropriate to his age, depending on the stepping stones of development that he can be expected to have reached. I am not going to give you a list of these because normal children vary so much. This means that when looking at the sort of list given in many books about babies and children you should not be depressed if your child does not seem to have reached a certain stage of development. The chances are that he will be ahead in some aspects of development and "behind" in others.

The doctor will test the way your baby uses his muscles to ensure that he moves from obtaining head control through sitting up, standing while holding on, and finally to standing on his own, and then to walking. The doctor will also check that he follows objects appropriately with his eyes, using smaller objects as he gets older. They will check his hearing too.

Some babies skip certain stages, while others remain longer at one stage before moving on to the next. Crawling is an example. If his mobility is fast and steady on four legs, what is the incentive to get up on two legs and keep falling over?

While a baby is progressing in one area, he sometimes seems to progress very little in another for a time. It is as though he is concentrating so much on one aspect of development that he ignores the other for a while. A child can be so excited by learning to babble and communicate that moving about takes second place.

All this will make interesting reading in your baby book, if you keep one, and when he is a parent your child will enjoy comparing his development with that of his own children.

Q Our baby has Down's Syndrome. Can we expect him to live to adulthood? Will there be a greater chance of any other children we may have being Down's babies, too? Are there any tests that we can have, and is the likelihood related to age? Whose advice should we seek?

Down's Syndrome babies used to be called "mongols" because of their Oriental facial appearance. But many parents were understandably upset by this word that suggested they were totally different from other babies. The correct approach is that Down's babies and Down's adults are people with a handicap.

A baby with Down's Syndrome and no associated problems, such as congenital heart disease, can be expected to live a fairly normal span of life. If he has heart disease, the outlook is the same as for anyone with this disorder and operative correction of the abnormality will remove the increased risk of an early death as a result of cardiac failure.

I remember meeting three charming Down's ladies over the age of sixty-five. The old concept that Down's babies die during childhood was grossly inaccurate, although it is true that in pre-antibiotic days, there was a greater chance of an early death because of the increased risk of infection. Life expectancy may be a little less than average, but from the practical point of view it helps to know they are likely to live an average span.

Intestinal obstruction at birth is more common in Down's babies but they will respond to the normal operative treatment.

Having had one Down's baby, you do have a greater chance that another baby will be similarly affected. This is dependent on your age and the type of chromosomal problem that has caused Down's Syndrome in your case.

All parents run a minimal risk of giving birth to a baby with Down's Syndrome whether or not there is a family history of an affected baby. If there is no family history, the risk is approximately 1 in 600 births. With increasing age of the mother, the risk increases greatly so that by the age of forty to forty-five years it becomes approximately 1 in 40 births.

To determine the likely cause in your case, your doctor can refer you to a geneticist who will then work out the probable risk in your family. The geneticist will not advise you either way about whether you should have another baby; that is for you and your husband to decide. He will merely give you his assessment of the risk for your family.

The good thing is that, if you become pregnant again, your doctor can tell, by testing the amniotic fluid that surrounds the baby in the uterus, whether your next baby has Down's Syndrome. This involves testing the chromosomes in the baby's skin cells that are shed into the fluid. Obviously, you would only undergo this amniocentesis—which involves a slight risk of producing a miscarriage—if you had made up your mind to have a termination of pregnancy should the test prove positive.

Q Our baby daughter was born with a cleft palate. Can you tell us what can be done about this?

I am sorry that your baby has a cleft palate, but glad that you do not mention an associated cleft lip which would mean the problem was more serious. A cleft lip and palate together are in fact more common than a cleft palate alone. Similarly, a cleft lip may occur on its own.

Naturally, the shock to parents is severe, and I always hope that doctors have photographs to show them the degree of success that can be achieved today by surgical repair. Photographs of another similarly affected baby showing the condition at birth and again after the operation are much more convincing than any amount of verbal explanation that a doctor or surgeon can give.

The operation required is usually undertaken by a plastic surgeon. He may see you for the first time while you are still in the hospital. Its timing depends to some extent on local arrangements but also on the preferences of the surgeon.

Your baby is likely to be under the care of a pediatrician in the early days when his main concern will relate to feeding and its problems. Having a cleft palate often causes swallowed milk to go into the nose as well as down the throat. Babies are much distressed by milk coming down the nostrils. This can often be prevented by feeding with a special cleft palate teat. This has a cowl on its upper surface that blocks the opening to the cleft.

An alternative is for an orthodontist (a specialist dentist) to make a plate that fits the baby's mouth and closes the cleft. Since the baby's mouth shape is changing with the rapid growth taking place, the plate will need to be changed every week or two in the early days. The plate helps equalize the two halves of the palate, if these are unequal, by stimulating the growth of the smaller side. This is more likely in association with a cleft lip.

Don't give up the idea of breastfeeding, however, because the plate will help. In any case not all babies with a cleft palate bring milk down the nose. If you are keen to breastfeed and there are problems in the early days, you can always be taught how to express the milk using an electric or hand pump or just the hands alone. After a few days, the baby may be able to feed normally without problems.

There are other methods of giving milk: the nipple of the bottle can be cut so as to provide two parallel slits at the end. Alternatively, spoon-feeding may be tried. The edges of the spoon will need to be bent over so that it becomes funnel-shaped and the milk is poured onto the back of the tongue.

The timing of the operation will be decided by the surgeon. He will be influenced by the size of the baby, who must be thriving. He will also check the baby's blood to be sure there is no anemia. It is likely that the baby will be about six months old, but some surgeons now operate shortly after birth.

Q **Our baby has a clubfoot. What has caused this? What can be done for it, and at what stage will any treatment be given?**

Clubfoot or *talipes*, to use its medical term, causes the foot to be misshapen and in most cases to be turned inwards. It was this disorder that affected Byron.

Most babies with a clubfoot are normal in every other way, the condition having resulted from compression while in the uterus. It is usual for both feet to be affected, although one may be worse than the other. The condition is obvious at birth.

Treatment starts as soon as is practical after birth and involves the use of pressure to get the foot back to a normal shape. In mild cases, manipulation by hand may be all that is needed. In severer cases, splints or plaster of Paris will be used. Results are excellent and very few cases require surgery. Special shoes are seldom needed and the legs are likely to be of equal length.

Q **Our baby has spina bifida. How will this affect her? Will the future necessarily be very bleak for her? What can be done with surgery?**

I am sorry to hear your baby has spina bifida but the future most certainly need not be bleak for her. It entirely depends on the type and site of the spina bifida, and whether your baby has any other problems as well.

I assume that your baby is newborn and that there is a visible abnormality of the spine. I mention this because the vertebral bones that comprise the spine and have failed to join in the middle in spina bifida can be so mildly affected that the skin overlaying the abnormal bones is normal. This condition is called *spina bifida occulta* (hidden) and in almost all cases there are no symptoms. It is discovered when the spine happens to be X-rayed, so that most of those affected go through life without even knowing that some of their vertebrae have not fully joined.

The problem comes when the skin overlying the spinal defect is involved. In mild cases, there is a cyst (*meningocele*) like a balloon, comprising only the coverings of the spinal cord—the large nerve that passes down the spine through the vertebrae. In severe cases, the spinal cord is exposed (*meningomyelocele*) causing a raw mauve area to be visible.

It is these severe cases that cause the problems because the nerves fail to develop properly so that the legs are usually paralyzed and the baby has no control over bowels or bladder. Added to this, there is a severe chance of associated *hydrocephalus* (water on the brain). The higher up the spinal defect, the worse the outlook. Spinal curvature is another serious association.

A surgeon can remove a meningocele, and the baby will then be normal because the spinal cord is not affected. With a meningomyelocele, the surgeon can repair the defect in the skin but cannot make the nerves normal, so the outlook is serious if paralysis is severe, because the child will be unable to walk normally and it is also more likely that he or she will die young.

Operations for hydrocephalus, whereby a tube is inserted that allows the extra water in the brain to drain away, are now remarkably successful, if the baby's head is of near normal size at birth.

Anyone who has given birth to a baby with spina bifida must be given information about the risks of having a recurrence in future pregnancies. The condition can now be diagnosed while the baby is still in the uterus.

From Baby to Toddler

Q Our son is now a year old and seems to show no inclination at all to walk. Is this something to be concerned about? Should we be seeking the advice of a specialist?

I can well understand your concern but many normal children do not walk until they reach eighteen months or even two years of age. The truly backward child shows delay in other areas of development as well, such as speech.

However, to set your mind at rest, consider these other areas of your child's development. First, does he sit up and can he get about by crawling? Children who crawl with skill are often late in walking simply because they see no reason for changing a secure method of movement on all fours to a shaky one on two legs only. Another group of later walkers are those children who have acquired the habit of "bottom-shuffling," a trait that often runs in families. Is he able to pull himself up to stand by holding onto a chair?

You should take his intellectual development into consideration as well. Is he babbling and even making single words? Does he show normal curiosity and has he developed manipulative skills? Has he gone through the stage of grasping objects with his whole palm and on to fine pincer movements with finger and thumb?

If he can do all these things in a normal fashion, then the fact that he is not yet walking, especially if he kicks his legs normally when lying down, does not matter. But if you have any lingering doubts, don't hesitate to check with your family doctor or pediatrician, who will be able to advise whether anything is wrong.

Try to avoid comparing his rate of development with that of other children. Even children from the same family show remarkably different rates of development and there is no constant sex difference for the development of these skills.

Q What would you suggest we do to encourage speech?

A child's reaction to under- or over-emphasis on speech is so delicately poised that, if a mother does not talk at all to her baby, he will be abnormally silent. Trying hard to make a child speak before he is ready and wants to do so may also result in refusal to speak.

Talking to babies is a most important way of encouraging early sounds, and your encouragement and enthusiasm for his achievement will make him babble still more. I once saw a six-month-old baby who was abnormally silent but not deaf. I realized his mother did not feel comfortable

Encourage your child to speak by talking to him or her as much as possible while you play. At the same time, try to avoid an overconcerned approach.

talking to him, and told her how important it was. I shall never forget her reply. "What! Talk to a baby? I couldn't do that. I could only talk to a dog!"

The parents who are most likely to over-encourage speech are those with a family history of speech problems. I have also come across this in parents who are on the stage and want their child to join the acting profession, too. A child's refusal to speak is a variety of negativism. He becomes a "word-holder," just as a child who is pressurized to have his bowels open becomes a "stool-holder."

Parents must adopt an unconcerned approach to their child's speech while at the same time talking to him in an ordinary way. No comment should be made if he doesn't answer. Parents who try to get words out of their child's mouth sometimes start to refuse to give him a toy he is wanting until he calls it by its correct name. The child then either says nothing or gives it the wrong name! Other parents tell their children to speak more slowly or more clearly, an approach that is virtually guaranteed to shut the child up. The correct approach, in addition to lack of concern, is to give the child the toy he is obviously wanting to play with and not make him say its name. Avoiding conflict prevents the development of the problem.

Parents must also be aware that early speech or vocalization is babble. The child is not yet old enough to form individual words because he can think faster than he can make his mouth work. As his skills develop, his babbling moves on to articulated speech with real words. Correction at this stage could cause the babble to persist as a stammer. It is therefore clear that talking to your child as you get on with your work encourages him to speak. Never use baby language since this forces your child to learn two words for an object instead of one.

Q **Our baby still has very little hair at nine months old. Could there be something wrong?**

I do not think there is anything wrong with your baby. The amount of hair varies greatly from one baby to another. Some are born with a large amount of hair, this being more common as well as more obvious in those with black hair. Other babies are born with very little hair.

In both instances, it is common for the hair to drop out during the early months of life and to be replaced with the permanent growth.

Your question does not lead me to think that your baby's hair is dropping out but that it is simply not growing as fast as with most babies. I believe it will gradually catch up in amount.

Q **Is it true that on the whole girls develop physically at a faster rate than boys?**

It is certainly true that puberty in girls occurs about two and one half years ahead of boys, so that there is both an earlier growth spurt and an earlier cessation of growth. Indeed, on the average, women end up six inches shorter than men.

However, I know of no evidence that girls develop faster in infancy. Such developmental differences are in any event always very difficult to prove because there are so many variables, each of which needs to be checked against a "control" in any scientific study. Thus the children included in any such survey would not only need to be born at the same time of year (this is because children grow faster in summer) but they would also need to come from similar social environments. But

studies have shown that there are certain racial differences. Black babies of *both* sexes develop faster than white babies for the first year or two of life; thereafter the differences in developmental rate even out.

This difference is very striking and was first observed by a research scientist, Dr. Rex Dean, not a pediatrician. Dr. Dean was working in the Medical Research Unit in Kampala, Uganda, and a French psychologist, Marcel Geber, tested his observations. These were found to be correct, and the results of their studies, first published in 1957, have been confirmed on many occasions.

Q **Is there really such a thing as growing pains?**

"Growing pains" are indeed a reality, but today the term "limb pains" is preferred since the pains have nothing to do with growth.

The child is healthy and is usually aged between three and seven years. The pain is felt in the limb muscles, especially the calves and thighs, not in the joints. Sometimes the child is awakened at night by pains that make him or her cry out. They are more common in the evening than in the morning. This is probably related to the cause, which is likely to be the nonstop activity of healthy children. A child doesn't slow up to go round corners! Small wonder then that his muscles ache at times.

An important aspect of management is parental confidence that the pain is not due to disease. Understandably, parents are often fearful that the pain is due to rheumatic fever but that condition affects joints and not muscles. Consequently, a sympathetic rub of the legs is usually all that is needed to make the pain go away.

It is essential for parents to be clear that, although the pain is not due to disease, it is very real. In other words, the child is not making it up.

Q **How can we get our three-year-old to sleep in a little longer? He wakes us every morning at about 5:30 a.m. and we then find it impossible to get back to sleep.**

It is important to see your very human question in terms of your comfort rather than your child's health. The only reason for getting a child to sleep is to give his parents a rest.

I imagine you have given your child sedatives and found that they don't work. I expect that, apart from telling him not to come into your room until you call him, you are also likely to have tried sending him to bed late, only to find that he goes to sleep in the living room!

The first step should be to look at the problem from *his* point of view. What is clear is that he does not need to sleep for as long at a stretch as you do. It is a misfortune that someone years ago listed the hours of sleep required by children of different ages. He was inaccurate and gave figures that were far too high. So he left parents feeling guilty if their children missed out on the supposed requirement of sleep for their particular age.

A normal child enjoys being awake. He will sleep when he wants to, but for the rest of the twenty-four hours he wants to explore the exciting world about him and to go on discovering new things every day. The problem comes when his sleep periods do not coincide with those of his parents. Consequently, they will send him to bed when he is in the middle of something of particular interest, and will tell him "to go to sleep." What an absurd expression! Have you ever been helped by someone telling you to go to sleep? Yet nurses do it to their patients every night in hospital, and sometimes even imagine their command has been obeyed.

Your child has had all the sleep he wants by 5:30 a.m. and now he wants you to play with him. Sleep is a difficult concept for a child to understand and the idea that this time you won't play with him when you do at other times must be difficult for him to comprehend. Normally, you are so gentle, but now you shout and tell him to go away.

Frankly, there is absolutely no alternative to his coming into your bed. After that, you might be lucky and find he goes to sleep, especially if loneliness was the main reason for his coming to your room, but he will certainly want you to play with him for part of the time.

Neighbors and relatives may tell you that if you let him come into your bed, this will become a habit and you won't get him out for years. They are talking nonsense. He wants to grow up, and once he is big enough to amuse himself he will enjoy playing in his own room, as long as there is no ban on his coming into your room on those occasions when he feels lonely and really needs to check that you are there.

Be sure to provide toys near his bed that he can reach without getting out. Choose those that might keep him interested for quite a time and that don't make a noise.

Not forcing him to bed at night may help, so let him play with you and watch television until you go to bed, if necessary. At least this means that he doesn't have to be in his room on his own and that no one has ordered him to go to sleep.

In practice, he will probably fall asleep on the floor or the sofa. Leave him there and save yourself the battle of putting him to bed against his will. Sleeping on the floor is not unhealthy.

I suspect it is sometimes very bright children who require less sleep. I remember a girl of three years with the same problem as your child. She was obviously an exceptionally bright child, falling into the "gifted" group. My first suggestion was to involve her brain more fully during the daytime. We agreed she should go to a nursery school, though at first the school would take her for mornings only because she might get too tired! I explained that the teachers would get tired before she did, which proved to be the case, but at least they agreed she could stay for the whole day.

Her brain was still working when she returned from school in the afternoon, so she also attended ballet school where she performed with intense activity. On returning home, she would go to bed, but by 4:00 a.m. she was knocking on her older brother's bedroom door, asking to be allowed in to play with him. When she was old enough for a formal intelligence test, her I.Q. was found to be 164, which is very high indeed.

I hope that I have persuaded you that your child may need less sleep than you and that the problem will sort itself out more quickly if you don't fight his desire to be awake.

Q Our three-year-old has a bad lisp. What can be done about this? Should he be seeing a speech therapist?

Lisping is normal when a baby is learning to talk. Those who go on lisping after the baby stage do it as a habit or because they are copying another child. A temporary lisp may also occur when a child has a gap from losing his front teeth. This explains why lisping results from an abnormal escape of air, causing sounds like *s* and *z* to be substituted by the sound *th*.

If your child has any of these forms of lisp, his way of speaking should be ignored and not corrected. However, you mention that it is severe, which is rare and can be due to partial deafness or a faulty action of the tongue. I would therefore consult your family doctor who is likely to refer you to a pediatrician. Deafness lies in the field of the audiologist and the ear, nose, and throat specialist. Additionally, the help of a speech therapist may be needed.

However, I must emphasize, in order to keep the subject in its proper perspective, that lisping in the vast majority of children is not serious and disappears when disregarded.

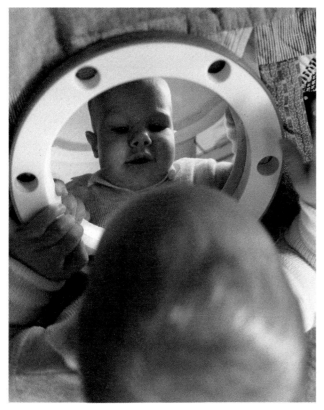

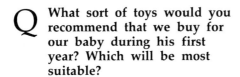

Through play, your infant will begin to learn many skills: but toys must be carefully chosen so that they are appropriate to age.

Q **What sort of toys would you recommend that we buy for our baby during his first year? Which will be most suitable?**

Rather than simply giving you a list of toys for an infant during the first year of life, I am also going to explain the principles of play as they apply during the early months.

Play by its very definition should be fun for a child, but it is also a serious activity, since it is through play that a child first learns many skills. It must therefore be appropriate for his age. Sometimes parents will encourage play by their mere presence, whereas at other times they will need actually to take part. Play should never be regarded as an activity to occupy a child so that his mother can get on with her work, although it is understandable that a parent may be tempted to use it this way at times.

During the first year, babies should have a string of safe toys firmly attached to hang across from one side of the crib to another. These should be very different so that they provide a variety of types of sensation such as color, feel, and noise. They should be brightly colored but the colors should differ. They should have different textures, some being plastic or wood, and others of different material. Some, but not all of them, should make noises and the sounds they emit should vary.

This string of toys will provide endless amusement for the baby, as long as it is placed within his reach, and the types of stimulation it offers are infinitely variable.

A child will first try to hold objects when he is about three months old, but he is unlikely to succeed until about six months old. At this age, he can probably grasp with his whole palm, and so a small brick will be most suitable. As he gets older, he will achieve a pincer movement between finger and thumb, thereby becoming able to hold smaller objects, too. This means you will have to be ready to remove some from his mouth because he will certainly be able to put them there in the second half of his first year.

Towards the end of his first year, he is likely to be able to crawl and therefore to play with objects on the floor. These need to be big, and

Try not to swamp your child with toys. Having too many things to play with may only be confusing to a toddler.

should run and roll. At first, he will be disappointed when they seem to disappear from his sight, although a toy that makes a noise even when stationary will be easier to find.

But your child will be thrilled most of all by playing with you, handing you objects and then taking them back, although to begin with he won't be able to let go. The essential is to avoid showing boredom, which means using subtlety in all sort of ways. Change his activities when he is losing interest, and also involve him when you are cooking or at the sink. If you enjoy his play and provide interesting activities, he will certainly enjoy it, too, but on no account flood him with toys since this will only bewilder him. One toy at a time is what he needs at this age so that he has time to find out as much as possible about it. And remember that *any* object he plays with is a "toy" to him. This means the whole range of safe household objects, too. Your wooden kitchen spoon is a lovely toy to bang and to stir with. Quite a number of his toys should be suitable for biting as well. Biting is only another aspect of exploration, and does not indicate anything vicious.

Q **So many of our friends' children have cupboards literally full of toys. Do children really need that many? Is it even possible for them to have too many?**

No, children do not need lots of toys. In fact, there is a disadvantage in swamping a child with toys. It can make it more difficult to decide which to play with so that they flit from one to another. Play requires concentration and parents need to understand that for children it is a serious activity. This is why I am constantly asking parents to avoid telling a child to clear his toys or paintings off the table because it is time for dinner. It is much better for a child to have his own table, or part of the main table, or to be encouraged to play on the floor.

All play is creative which is why it combines fun and learning. Modern toy designers are skilled and imaginative artists who are able to think like a child.

Parents who flood their children with toys are unlikely to be aware of their importance. Toys are merely seen as a bribe to keep a child quiet. Some parents visiting their children in the hospital feel obliged to give a new toy at every visit. Consequently, the toys are not valued, nor their possible use fully explored and exploited.

Q Is teething really very painful? Could that be why our baby seems so fretful?

I have often wondered how this concept arose, and feel it must be the result of the pain felt by adults when they have an impacted wisdom tooth. But I am glad to say that dental students are now taught that the eruption of normal teeth does not cause pain.

I am constantly trying to persuade parents that teething only produces teeth. It is true that the gum overlying an erupting tooth may look red, but that is not to say that it is causing pain. Sometimes the cheek on the same side as the erupting tooth also looks red.

As long as your approach to teething is to disregard it as a problem, you will find that your child's teeth erupt without any difficulty. Indeed, you will probably just happen to notice from time to time that another tooth has arrived without any associated symptoms.

The greatest danger is to ascribe illness to teething. In days gone by, the eruption of teeth was given as a cause of fever, constipation, or convulsions. Nothing was further from the truth, and I fear that some children may even have died because a diagnosis of teething was given when really they had a very serious illness.

Teething, therefore, does not in itself cause your child to be fretful; so if he *is* fretful, you will have to look elsewhere for the cause. It is interesting that parents and, I fear, some doctors and nurses, only ascribe such symptoms to teething when they occur in very young children. Yet the second dentition is not complete until about the age of fourteen. If an eight-year-old were to throw a brick through a window, I don't believe that you would say "Poor fellow, he's teething."

Q Do you think that small children really need an afternoon nap? Does this stop them from sleeping through the night?

Since you put the question as strongly as you have, I find myself wanting to answer that children do not need an afternoon nap. Certainly no harm would come to them if they missed a nap. If a child needs to sleep for an hour or so

in the afternoon, he will certainly do so. The interesting thing is that because parents mostly don't feel too concerned about whether a child sleeps in the afternoon or not, they take the pressure out of the whole business. Consequently, unlike nighttime, the child is not told to go to sleep, doesn't have to fight against his parents' wishes, and may well drop off very easily.

I would therefore judge the answer to your question by your child's own behavior patterns. If he is obviously tired out, let him lie on the sofa and he will probably go straight to sleep. On the other hand, another child is so bursting with energy and curiosity that he just hasn't got time to go to sleep. I have a hunch that it is the brighter child who doesn't want a great deal of sleep because he has so much he wants to do that he can't switch off. If that is the case with your child, on no account try to make him turn off. The concept of being overtired is not one that fits my idea of how a child's body works if it is left to adjust to its own needs.

Having an unnecessary nap may affect his nighttime cycle so that he doesn't want to sleep when his parents expect him to do so. Parents may therefore try to stop their child from going to sleep in the daytime if they are especially concerned about his sleeping at night. This does not seem to work, however, and it is often the case that the child merely becomes irritable because his body knows that it needs a temporary switch-off.

The more I work with children, the more amazed I am by how they work out their own needs, if only adults do not interfere too greatly. The amount of sleep required by a young child is extremely variable and many need less than adults. Some children are made to have an afternoon nap to give their mother or care-giver a rest. This seems perfectly reasonable, but of course the child may stay awake longer at night.

Q Our four-year-old seems to have a bit of a stammer. Should we seek expert advice about this before he starts school? Would speech therapy be helpful at this stage?

During the first years of life, all children pass through a babbling phase before they are able to change early vocalization noises into words. Some parents become worried by this perfectly normal phase, mistaking it for a stammer, especially if there is a family history of stammering, and react by telling their child to speak more slowly and more clearly. The child then becomes self-conscious and, in trying to do as his parents want, may begin to stammer. The answer is for parents to let this normal stage pass without comment—not an easy task since parents have a natural wish to do something active.

Your task will now be to help your son gain confidence in speech. When he is stammering, don't help him with words but help him with action if you know what he is asking for. Have no fear that this will make him lazy; it will help him relax instead of struggling to make himself understood. If this approach succeeds, speech therapy will not be required. But if he has begun to make facial grimaces and even bodily contortions in his attempts to speak, speech therapy is essential.

Q **My husband and I are uncertain whether both our baby's testicles are down. What should we do about this?**

Since you have doubts, it is essential that you see your doctor who will check that both testicles are in the scrotum. This is not always as easy as it sounds because, during the early months of life, testicles are "retractile." This means that they can be pulled up into the lower part of the abdomen by a small muscle in the scrotum. This particularly occurs when the inside of the thigh is tickled.

The fundamental rule that doctors make is whether the testicle can be brought down into the scrotum. If this is the case, then one can be quite sure that the testicle will descend naturally and that it is behaving in this retractile fashion.

If one or both of the testicles is absent from the scrotum and not of the retractile type described, then it is up to the doctor to see if he can find where the testicle is lying. The testicle is most often in what is termed the "superficial inguinal pouch." This is an abdominal extension of the scrotum, lying under the skin, but superficial to the muscles. If you place your little finger at the lower end of the scrotum and push it inwards so that the finger goes up inside the scrotum, you will find that it continues on into this pouch. Having found the testicle in the pouch, the doctor then tries to bring it down into the scrotum. The testicle may be tethered in the pouch, but most often with warm hands in a warm room, he will find he can do this. Provided it can reach the upper part of the scrotum, the testicle is likely to descend completely on its own, although your doctor will want to check this from time to time.

If your family doctor has any doubts about the position of the testicle and whether it is undescended, he will refer your child either to a pediatrician or directly to a pediatric surgeon.

The specialist will check the same points. If he finds that the testicle is definitely undescended and cannot be brought down into the scrotum, he will arrange an operation to bring it down. This is usually carried out between the ages of two and three, and certainly by the age of four. The main aim is that the testicle should be in position when the child goes to school. It is known that testicles seldom descend on their own after the age of twelve months, and in fact very few of them come down on their own after the age of a few weeks.

Occasionally, neither testicle can be felt. In that case, the doctor will do some tests to check aspects of the baby's sex. He will almost certainly arrange to operate in order to bring down the testicles if they have a long enough cord to reach the scrotum.

The condition of undescended testicles is painless. The operation will cause some natural soreness but is not going to give your child a great deal of pain. It is, of course, very important that testicles should be in the scrotum since undescended testicles can lead to sterility.

The operation is likely to be done under a general anesthetic, but many pediatric surgeons will operate on an outpatient basis, meaning that your child will be able to go home in the evening. He will only have a simple dressing in the groin where the cut is made. The dressing will keep the scar from being soiled, but be sure to ask the surgeon whether you can bathe the baby.

Q **Is it true that the age at which the first teeth appear is related to a child's potential intelligence? Which teeth usually erupt first, and when?**

The timing of tooth eruption has nothing to do with intelligence. This is just one more of those many myths that surround childhood.

The first tooth to erupt in the first dentition is a central incisor, at about six months of age. The first incisor to appear is usually in the lower jaw rather than in the upper. This is a biting tooth, whereas the molars that lie behind and are chewing teeth do not usually appear before the end of the first year.

Although the age of six months is the average time for the first tooth to appear, variation in time of eruption is great as in everything else that happens with babies. Some babies are born with a tooth present, while others have none until they are a year old. This is not a cause for concern, except that a tooth present at birth may be poorly fixed and may require removal lest it come out on its own and is inhaled into the lungs.

Left There is no evidence to show that the age at which teeth first erupt is related in any way to intelligence, nor that teething as such causes pain. So if your child seems fretful, don't ascribe the distress to teething but look elsewhere for the cause. Right As a perfectly normal stage of development, known as the "oral phase", your infant will begin to use his mouth as a means of exploring objects. You will therefore need to keep small toys and beads well out of reach in case he should choke on them. Far right It is not a good idea to encourage your child to use one hand rather than the other. Many problems resulted in the past when parents tried to force their toddlers to use their right hands rather than their left.

The presence of teeth does not cause pain on breastfeeding because the baby is sucking and not biting. Moreover, the tongue covers the lower teeth in order to assist sucking.

The first tooth of the permanent dentition to appear is a premolar at the age of six years. It is therefore termed the "six-year molar".

Q **Our fourteen-month-old son is always pulling things in his mouth. We are terrified that he might inhale or swallow something like a small toy or bead for instance. If that were to happen, what should we do? Can you describe the action we should take?**

It is a natural stage in a child's development for him to put objects into his mouth. This habit usually starts at about six months of age and heralds the "oral phase" of development. At that age, the mouth is the most interesting part of the body to the child. He puts objects into his mouth to learn more about them and because he enjoys their feel.

Putting small toys and beads in the mouth can be prevented only by keeping them away. For this reason, cheap toys should be avoided because small pieces may easily come off.

If he should choke on an inhaled object, your actions must be rapid because of the risk of asphyxia. One of two methods is used. The first maneuvre is to hold the child upside down by the feet and slap his back. But there is a danger that this could in fact force the object further down. In the alternative method, known as the Heimlich maneuvre, the lower end of the chest is compressed with both hands. The clasped hands are jerked inwards, forcing the breast bone towards the backbone. This causes air to be forced out of the lungs and hopefully the inhaled object is blown out as well.

If an inhaled object is not removed by either maneuvre described above, it is likely that it

has passed the junction of the two lungs immediately below the vocal chords. This situation is an emergency, and the child should be taken at once to a hospital where a doctor will use a long tube known as a bronchoscope. The object is then grasped with long pincers that are inserted through the tube while the child is anesthetized.

Fortunately, most swallowed objects are sufficiently small to be passed in the stools. It is always surprising how even coins that look large on an X-ray can manage to get out of the stomach, the point at which the object may stick. There is understandable concern if a child swallows some pointed object, the commonest being a safety pin. But many such objects pass without causing problems because the sharp parts get covered by intestinal contents. Therefore, if the child is well, it is better to do nothing— except, of course, to check each stool to know if the object has been passed. If a swallowed object is very small, you need not even call your doctor, but for a larger object, it is definitely best to go to the hospital emergency department, where they will almost certainly X-ray the child. As long as he remains well, the doctor will want to X-ray the abdomen again after a day or so, and will be able to check whether the object is moving along the intestinal canal.

When the child remains well, I always hope that the hospital doctor will allow the child to be observed by his parents at home rather than being admitted to the hospital. The role of the parents is to report any change in behavior or whether the child

becomes ill. This will be much more obvious if the child is not admitted to the hospital, because admission would add another variable if the child is upset or lonely. The good thing is the rarity with which a pin perforates the wall of the intestine, and even when this happens, the child does not rapidly become ill. This is one other reason why parents at home are likely to notice any changes more readily than hospital staff who have never met the child before.

He can be fed in the ordinary way. In the past, children used to be given sandwiches containing cotton wool, in the hope of covering sharp points, but this is very upsetting to a child and probably makes little difference.

Q Our baby seems always to pick up things with his left hand. Is this a sign that he will definitely be left-handed? Should we be encouraging him to use his right hand instead?

It is at about the age of six to seven months that a baby first starts to pick up objects. He does this with his hand in a grasp postion so that all the fingers remain touching. He may then bring the other hand into use to help the first and to make it less likely for the object to be dropped. At this stage, he will pick up an object with either hand indiscriminately—in other words, he is ambidextrous. As soon as he has picked something up with one hand, he is likely to pass it to the other. He is also likely to put it in his mouth.

As the months go on, he becomes able to undertake a pincer movement between forefinger and thumb. Over the next three months, it gradually becomes obvious that he is using one hand more than the other, until finally you are certain whether he is righthanded or lefthanded.

On no account should you try to encourage him to use one hand rather than the other. If he is lefthanded, then of course he must remain so. It was a sad time when, in the past, parents and others tried to force their children to be righthanded, and many problems resulted.

However, if a baby of about seven months is very obviously using one hand only whereas he would be expected to be ambidextrous, it is likely that there is something wrong with the hand he is not using.

Q I am breasfeeding my new baby and my three-year-old insists on feeding from the other breast at the same time. What should I do? Is it something to worry about?

This is a common happening, not a problem as such. Looked at through the child's eyes, it's perfectly normal. You have a new baby and feed him contentedly at your breast, so why should it be wrong for *him* to do so?

Treat the whole episode in a matter-of-fact manner and your child will soon get bored and want to play instead. But if you scold him and try to prevent him breastfeeding, you may be in for trouble. He will not only try to feed on every possible occasion but will probably manage to embarrass you in front of others.

Children are past masters at exploiting situations. One mother told me how she did nothing to stop her older child from sucking at the breast; he took one swig, made a face, and spat out the milk!

Q How important is it, do you think, for a small child to have his own room? Is it wrong for the sexes to share?

It is ideal for a child to have his or her room as long as this happens at the right age, which varies with every child. A newborn baby, however, needs to be with his parents like every other animal, and I hope he is allowed into their bed at

times, too.

Children both need and want to grow up, and having your own bedroom with your name on the door is one way of doing so. It is also a private area where you can play on your own. This is why babies who sleep in the family bed don't stay there forever! Handled properly, they look forward enormously to moving to their own room, especially if they have been allowed to choose some of the decorations, and best of all have done some of the paintwork. A few children do like to share, and certainly this is true of twins.

Of course, not all families live in a house that is large enough for each child to have his own bedroom, but bunks are exciting and a very clever substitute for one's own room. There's no need to segregate the sexes until puberty, and by then they will want to be on their own, anyway.

Q How can we best discourage our three-year-old daughter from demanding candy all the time?

So many parents speak about candy as though it is something that must be available. The answer is simply not to have any candy in the house. If you start off this way, your problems will be far fewer.

I appreciate that a child is likely to be given candy at parties, for instance. However, your basic approach should be that candy is very damaging to the teeth, and you love your child too much to allow this to happen.

Obviously, any approach in which candy is used as a bribe or a reward would totally negate this.

Q Lisa, who is four years old, seems very small for her age by comparison with other children in the playgroup. Is this something to be concerned about? Or is it likely that she will catch up in size before too long?

You will really have to ask your doctor about this, because only by checking your daughter's height on a standard chart can it be determined whether or not she falls within the average range of height for her age.

An allowance will, of course, be made for the height of you both, as Lisa's parents. Short parents tend to produce short children and special height charts are therefore available that allow for "mid-parental height," obtained by calculating the mid-point between the height of both parents.

If such tests leave your doctor still uncertain,

he or she will probably refer your daughter to a pediatrician, who is naturally an expert in growth. It is most likely that he will be able to explain that all is well, even though she is possibly growing more slowly than average. But if there are any doubts, he or she will carry out special tests, particularly to check that there is no problem affecting those glands that control growth.

Exceptionally, it may be discovered that there is a deficiency of growth hormone that is manufactured by the pituitary gland. The good news is that this can now be replaced by injections of pituitary gland extract containing human growth hormone.

Q **Is it true that becoming "clean" is easier for a child than becoming "dry"?**

It is easier at all ages to control the bowels than to control urine. Passing urine is so simple that a child absorbed in his play may not realize it has happened until the flow of urine has begun. He may not even notice it, although his mother may be aware that he has grabbed hold of his penis. Passing stools requires a degree of straining and is much more obvious so that a parent has time to produce a potty for him to sit on.

Passing urine happens so much more often. Soiling is more uncomfortable than wetting. Few children object to wet pants but many, especially girls, dislike dirty pants. Staying dry all night is asking a lot of a young child in terms of time, compared with staying clean. Passing urine requires minimal muscle power whereas you have to strain to have the bowels open. Tightening the muscles that keep the anus closed is simpler than shutting off the urethra, the canal leading from the bladder to the exterior.

Lastly, a full bladder can be stretched very little whereas a full rectum can more easily be widened, and there is also the intestine above (the colon) that can hold a great deal more.

Q **Our child is almost four years old, but she has recently started to wet the bed again at night. Should we seek medical advice about this? Could you tell us if the bed-wetting is likely to have a physical or psychological cause?**

So many normal children are still wet at the age of three that my first inclination is to suggest doing nothing except to take the pressure off,

because something has probably happened to make her lose confidence.

It's the fact that she has already achieved being dry that makes the difference, especially if she has any associated symptoms such as pain on passing urine or extreme frequency that could indicate an urinary infection. Doctors work to a golden rule that if a child has started to wet after becoming dry they must exclude an anatomical abnormality of the kidney system. This means special X-rays—an intravenous pyelogram (IVP) that shows up the whole system and, possibly on a separate occasion, a micturating cystogram. In this test, the liquid that will show up on the X-ray is injected into the bladder and the child asked to pass urine. The radiologist is then able to check whether there is any back flow from the bladder to one or both kidneys.

The most likely reason, however, is an emotional cause. Perhaps she has just started nursery school or has had a new baby brother or sister? These are very big happenings in a child's life. They make the child feel less safe, and one of the normal reactions to being worried is to pass urine more often.

Q **At what age do you recommend a child is taught to swim?**

The straightforward answer to your question is that I hope children are taught to swim very early on. By that I mean babies should experience water play with their parents from about the age of two to three months.

This is not so much in order to get them to swim at an early age as to give them the wonderful experience of another environment while still feeling safe with their parents. But the whole family must be under the supervision of a very experienced teacher in early swimming.

We have been using hydrotherapy with normal and handicapped babies at Charing Cross Hospital in order that the parents can experience the intimacy that being in the water together brings. Of course, the handicapped children have the added benefit of the buoyancy provided by the water.

Having experienced this intimacy and new form of movement, the parents and the baby can enjoy play that allows them to separate while still in view of each other. The baby will not experience fear and will achieve movements that most children without this water experience in infancy do not reach until a much later age.

All babies should experience as many opportunities to play and move as possible. Being in water will inevitably lead to independent swimming, just as every normal baby experiences learning to stand and then to walk.

The striking aspect is the tremendous fun experienced by the babies and their parents. Obviously, the more that parents and children do together, the better. Through water play, which provides a new form of amusement, the family will find one more way of enjoying each other.

Q **I have rather ugly feet—due, I suspect, to wearing shoes that were too tight when a teenager. How can we best ensure our baby's feet develop well? Is it a good idea to let him go without shoes and socks as much as possible?**

I do not suggest that there is anything special for you to do to ensure your baby's feet are going to develop well, apart from making sure that shoes are not too tight. Most importantly, this goes for socks as well.

It is now felt that babies should not be given shoes until they start to walk, and that the more opportunities they have to go without shoes, the better. This ensures that the developing feet are able to move freely.

Q **How will we recognize the right time to start toilet training? Is it harmful to start too early?**

Babies are usually to ready to start toilet training at the age of two to three years. By this time they are willing to sit on the potty without complaint and it will not be long before they fetch the potty themselves when they want to use it. You will need to continue with diapers at night for some time longer.

If, however, your baby has been trained at an early age, he may react in a negative way and refuse to cooperate. A hundred years ago, tiny babies of a few weeks old were placed on their potties on an adult's lap. The babies would respond by passing urine and stools as a conditioned reflex, just like Pavlov's dogs, the reflex being set in motion by the rim of the pot touching the baby's bottom.

This method saves laundry and would be ideal if it was not followed by potty-refusal at between one and one-and-a-half years of age in many babies; the child refuses to sit on the potty, his mother makes the mistake of forcing him to do so, and the stage is set for a battle as the child refuses to let go of his urine or stools. Eventually, the mother gives in and puts him in his diaper which is the signal to the child to pass his urine or a stool. He no longer has to fight and so naturally lets go.

The principal danger of starting toilet-training too early is that a child may react in a negative way, refusing to cooperate. It is important that your child does not discover an anxiety on which he or she can play.

Try not to make a big thing about your child having his bowels open. Some parents lavish praise on a child so that the stool almost becomes an object of worship. Then, lo and behold, the mother throws it into the lavatory and flushes it away. This is one more example of how difficult it is for a child to understand the behavior of adults. A moment ago, the child believed the stool to be very important and himself to be very clever. The next moment, his mother throws away what he has produced.

Provided you play it calmly, a child will get pleasure from a decorative potty chair. But be careful he knows what it is for, so that he does not think you have provided him with an engine on which to skid around the floor. Many children also enjoy being grown up and using the adult toilet with a special seat.

As in all aspects of child rearing, do everything you can to ensure that the child does not discover another of your anxieties on which he can play. It doesn't matter how old he is when he achieves this control, so make sure you don't fall into the trap of competing with your neighbors. The use of the word "clean" signals this aspect. Don't refer to your child as being "clean" as though all the others are dirty.

Bear in mind, too, that some children need to get out of diapers and training pants to achieve this stage. Diapers are for wetting and soiling, so it is not really surprising that some children have to move on to the next stage of clothing before understanding what is expected of them.

Q **From time to time, I get the feeling that our toddler is overtired. He gets restless and very excited. Could that be the case and, if so, how can we best prevent it happening? I doubt he would sleep for any longer than he does now. So how can we calm him down during the day?**

The concept that a toddler becomes "overtired" is not one that I share. In fact, young children have the great good fortune of being able to go to sleep whenever they feel like it. You only have to look around you—for example, in a restaurant or in a park—and you will see that lots of the children have just nodded off to sleep.

You have used the label "overtired" to describe a child who is restless and excited. I must therefore work out with you *why* your child is restless and excited, and let us not put it down to your term "overtired." It is, of course, natural for young children to be excited at times. This is normal behavior. Unfortunately, fairly recently, the word "hyperactivity" has come into use, as though it was a special form of behavior instead of the common behavior of most children at times.

For this reason, I do not give such children a special diet, leaving out certain food additives, as has sometimes been recommended, because there is no solid evidence that this makes any difference. A few children who are "hyperactive" are reacting this way because they have a behavior problem. For example, children react negativistically if they are always being told *not* to do something. The important thing is for you to work out, with your doctor's help if necessary, whether your child's activity is normal or whether he is exhibiting negativistic behavior.

Many parents whose children are very active are worried in case this is due to poor mental development. It is true that children who are mentally handicapped may be very wild and active. However, it is unlikely that your child is mentally handicapped because he is so normal for most of the time.

I agree with you that you should not try to get him to sleep for longer than he does now because he is sleeping the amount that he needs. If you were to try to *make* him go to sleep, it would have exactly the opposite effect. Try turning the pressure off, because calm behavior from you causes a similar response from him. A skillful choice of play together can work wonders.

Q **How can we best explain to Julia—she's three years old— how dangerous it can be to speak to or to go off with strangers? You hear such dreadful stories.**

Since your daughter is only three years old, I cannot really believe that you will be letting her out of your sight, so she is unlikely to be in danger from strangers. Certainly, you should not do so because she is too young to understand any explanation of the risks involved.

By the age of about five years, she might be the sort of child who wanders into the street, putting herself at risk, especially if she looks on everyone as a friend. Obviously, your fear is not the talking to strangers but the fact that this could lead to her accepting an invitation to go off with a stranger. It will be difficult for her to understand that she *can* talk to strangers when you are with her especially if you have told her to be polite and to say "Hello" when you meet a friend who is a stranger to *her*. The basic points that I would aim to get over are first of all that she talks to strangers only when with her parents or your approved care-giver whom she knows. Secondly, she must never accept a gift such as candy from a stranger. Lastly, she must never accept an invitation from a stranger to go for a walk or a ride.

She is bound to find these instructions strange, especially if you have emphasized the need to be friendly, but her implicit faith in you and the serious way you repeatedly explain the message will make her realize the importance of what you are saying.

She won't appreciate the whys and wherefores, so don't even try to get her to understand because you are bound to get her confused. Simply explain the rule, but answer in the simplest language any questions she asks about your reasons.

The Family Circle

Q Do you think that small children should be encouraged to help their parents around the house?

I would encourage children to help at home in every way possible. They enjoy these activities because they want to please their parents. However, it is essential that they are not made to feel they are being made to do a chore. It is reasonable that children help with housework, but if you call it housework and make it a duty, they will soon come to hate it.

I remember how much our four-year-old enjoyed using the lawn mower, to the extent that he would manage to mow a very large area of lawn, under supervision. No pressure was put on him, and he thoroughly enjoyed the activity until he was about eight years old, when he realized that he was working and not playing!

A child will also find it much more fun to be undertaking these activities with his mother or father, rather than on his own. To be sent upstairs to tidy your room is very boring, and you are unlikely to take much trouble over it.

Some parents will be wondering whether this sort of activity should be rewarded. I think it is a pity if a point is reached where the child expects to be paid for what he does at home. The occasional gift will be much appreciated, but unless the whole aspect of rewards is handled wisely, the child could adopt a form of blackmail, leading to other problems.

By all means, encourage a child to help around the house: but safety should be the watchword.

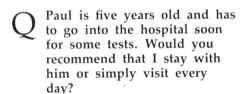

Q Paul is five years old and has to go into the hospital soon for some tests. Would you recommend that I stay with him or simply visit every day?

For the first five or six years of life, I think it is important to stay with your child if you can, unless of course he is very definite in that he does not want you around because he feels grown up. However, quite frankly, few children of five would feel that confident about going into the hospital.

If a choice of the hospital came into it, I would always choose the one that encouraged a mother or father to stay. The effect of separation during a hospital stay has been the subject of various reports internationally, but sadly, even today, not all hospitals make provisions for a parent to stay. The common argument is that a hospital does not have sufficient facilities, but my experience is that mothers and fathers will accept no end of discomfort in order to be with their young

children in the hospital. Being with the child is the all-important point. A parent doesn't want a well-equipped bedroom on a different floor. How much better to sleep beside the child on a folding bed, whether the child is in a ward or a cubicle.

In practice, I have not found this too difficult to organize. If the ward gets too crowded, we use an adjoining playroom and convert it into a dormitory. My experience is that parents do not complain as long as they are allowed to stay, and so the whole thing inevitably hinges to a great extent on the cooperation of both the medical and the nursing staff.

One last point: while you are checking about beds for parents, find out if the pediatric department has a preparation program for children due to be admitted. Coming to the ward in advance just to learn something about hospital life can be a tremendous help—to children and parents alike.

Q I am about to have my first child and am concerned as to how my dog will react to the baby. He often shows signs of jealousy when my nephew visits us.

You are right to be concerned, and on no account should you leave them in the same room even if things seem tranquil enough. The baby might happen to make a noise that could give the dog a shock so that he reacts in a sudden, uninhibited manner.

Your basic approach should be the same as with a jealous older child. Be sure not to reduce your affection for the dog, and continue to spend time with him. Above all, don't let him detect your anxiety because anxiety is catching with dogs as well as with humans. Let the dog meet the baby in the ordinary course of events rather than making a special occasion of the first encounter.

Hopefully, all will go well and you will have no trouble. But if there are any signs that your dog might hurt or bite the baby, be sensible. You must immediately find your dog an alternative home.

Q Could I be a danger to my baby? I am very worried because just occasionally, his incessant crying really gets the better of me and I feel like shaking him.

Your feelings are very understandable and are felt by many mothers, but you are wise to ask the question. The answer has to be that you *could* be a danger to your baby, though the fact that you have thought about the risk lessens it. I am sure that many mothers have said to you that they have had the same feelings at times. But that doesn't really help unless you understand why you feel this way and how it is that most mothers don't actually harm their babies.

Even the most capable of mothers can be driven to distraction by an infant's continuous crying, especially if she is feeling overwhelmed and depressed by the amount of work it takes to look after a baby. Add to that the loneliness often involved, particularly for those living in a big-city apartment with few friends and a large family to care for. So much depends, too, on having a sympathetic and understanding partner who gets home from work as early as possible and relieves you of as much of the burden as he can. For those mothers on their own, the problem may be even more harsh.

But the most influential factor as to whether or not you actually shake or hit your baby is your own childhood. If you were brought up in a caring atmosphere by parents who loved you and a mother who mothered you, you will be able to do the same for your children. On the other hand, if you had a deprived childhood, the ability to mother and to tolerate the strains will be less.

A crying baby cannot be spoiled and should always be picked up and cuddled, unless his mother is so strained that she knows she might shake him. Under these circumstances, the normal mother puts him safely in his cot and goes away to make herself a cup of coffee or tea and relax. The deprived mother, however, feels unable to do this. In extreme cases it is almost as though her baby is telling her that she is a rotten mother. This mother needs help. If this is how *you* feel, you must see that you discuss the matter with your doctor, social worker, or whoever is close, sympathetic, and able to be a good listener as well as understanding the problem.

Q We are thinking of employing a child-minder. What qualities do you suggest we should look for in whoever we employ?

You are right to be thinking so carefully about the sort of person for such an important task. Basically, a child-minder has to take on all the caring aspects that a mother would provide and yet she must not usurp the mother nor make the mother feel inadequate. Children need to feel that she is someone who helps their mother but not a second mother. The child-minder, meanwhile, has the difficult task of not becoming possessive for their affection. If she does, the children may exploit the situation, causing conflict between the parents and the child-minder, and confusion for the children.

I think the most suitable characteristics are likely to be found in a young girl who is experienced with children and, best of all, one who comes from a large and loving family herself. A young girl is also more likely to accept the views of the parents on how their child is to be brought up rather than dominating them with her own ideas.

Obviously you will need to check on her competence in looking after children. If she has worked as a child-minder already, you would be wise to talk to her previous employers. Both you and your husband must also like her as a person, and you will all need to agree on your basic approaches to bringing up children. A rigid disciplinarian will cause problems, unless that is your approach to bringing up children, in which case I hope you will change! Similarly, her approach to punishment should be the same as yours so that the children cannot play off one of you against the other.

If you are going to be away all day and perhaps

for several days at the stretch, you will need someone very experienced both to run the home and to look after the children. In that case, a fully trained child-minder would be a wise choice. On the other hand, if it is a matter of being able to take over completely for short periods only whenever necessary and for the rest of the time to assist you, I would suggest a mother's helper or an au pair who is competent to do just that. Whether or not she lives with the family will depend on your wishes and your outside commitments.

Q **What can we reasonably expect of our two-year-old at mealtimes? Should manners be taught at this age?**

Mealtimes are family occasions that should be encouraged. Therefore, I very much hope you eat together. However, you will need to watch that your child does not exploit the situation, causing battles with you because you have definite ideas as to how he should behave. Don't force him to sit still because this is difficult for young children. If he chooses to have a short run around, don't stop him.

Children are very clever at drawing their parents into conflict. If this happens, his behavior should be ignored so that your child fails to draw you into what is a method of testing you.

It is very important not to expect "good" behavior at a very early stage. A child will readily use any form of behavior that he realizes causes you to be upset. He is bound to be messy and to drop food on the floor, but handle this without comment.

Adults meet for meals as social occasions, and this should also apply to young children who can gradually learn the niceties of manners by copying good behavior, without being forced. Remember that mealtimes should be enjoyable for adult and child.

Q **Do you think that an eight-hour flight is too much for a three-year-old? We are planning to go abroad for two weeks next summer.**

On the whole, children make good travelers, as long as you prepare well for the trip. You will probably find that your three-year-old hardly notices the flight if you keep him occupied. It is you, the parents, I am sorry for because an eight-hour flight is tiring without children, let alone with them.

Bring an in-flight bag containing appropriate toys, especially drawing books, as well as simple games. Take every opportunity the airline staff offer to amuse him, too. Even at three, your child may be invited to the flight deck. It is quite safe for him to walk about and other passengers are likely to enjoy his company for a short time and may keep him occupied.

When booking, be sure to tell the travel agent the age of your child so that you get the best facilities available. Check whether there are special arrangements for children at the airport. Parents are often not told that there are nurseries at some airports. Children and those accompanying them are usually allowed to board first.

I would not suggest you bring special food, unless your child is on a diet. He will eat what he wants. Don't try to make him eat more because meals seem to come around so often.

Young children usually sleep soundly on a plane, so even if *you* don't get much rest, the chances are that your toddler will arrive as fresh as a daisy.

Q **Having recently remarried, I am wondering what my three-year-old should call my new husband. She sees her real father, whom she calls Daddy, only once every three months or so, as he is working abroad. We are anxious to avoid confusion at this rather difficult time.**

This is an important question but the answer should be left to your daughter. She will probably use the same name for him as you do at first, and you should accept her right to decide what she calls her stepfather. Later, she may prefer to call him Daddy, either because he has earned that position in her eyes or because she has no wish to indicate a difference to her school friends. She will base her decision on how she feels about the two men in her life, and though her real father may feel hurt by her calling her stepfather Daddy, he must accept her right to call people by the name she feels most appropriate. It is most unlikely she will call them both Daddy but instead she may invent some subtle way of differentiating them.

The worst error you could make would be to make the decision for her. I remember an instructive conversation with my three children when I asked them if they would prefer to call my wife and myself by our first names. They were very definite that they would *not*. Anyone, they said, could use our first names but only *they* had the right to call us Mommy and Daddy.

The small child who is mature enough to leave his mother's skirts will definitely benefit from mixing with other children at a playgroup, nursery school or daycare center. It must be a parental decision, however, as to whether the child is ready to gain from the new experience.

Q **Is it worthwhile sending our three-year-old to playschool? She seems very happy and contented at home. But we do wonder if there could be advantages in her being with other children.**

I like to think that every young child is given optimal opportunities for full development in all areas. It sounds as though you are providing all that your child needs, because I get the feeling that you are with her most of the day and that you understand her need for play in its widest sense, and are providing this.

What, then, could playschool offer that you are not already providing? It's interesting that you use the word "playschool," which is an ideal description although not an official term. What are the alternatives? Playgroups are usually run by mothers, some being ex-teachers, while all should have taken a course on the needs of young children and how to organize such a group. You may find yourself more involved if you choose a playgroup rather than a nursery school, although professional nursery schools do appreciate parental involvement. Attendance at a playgroup is likely to be on the basis of, say, three mornings a week, and can thus combine well with home activities.

The alternative—a nursery school or preschool—is usually a full-time establishment, although some children may attend for morning or afternoon sessions only. A teacher will be in charge, and she may be helped by other trained teachers and by aides. The school will usually be open from 9:00 a.m. to 3:30 p.m. with normal school holidays. Sometimes the teacher in charge will also encourage mothers to help at the school on a rotating basis, which I feel is a good idea because they can learn so much about handling children as well as getting lots of new ideas for play.

The daycare center, a third possibility, is open all year round. A good daycare center may have all the assets of a nursery school but will be provided primarily for working mothers. There are often fairly long waiting lists.

Armed with this information, I suggest that you visit playgroups and nursery schools in your area. In the final analysis, it will be for you to decide whether your child will enjoy and gain by the experience. Taking part in activities with other children is a useful addition to what you are already doing at home.

As long as your child is ready for this wider world and mature enough to leave your skirts (although you are likely to be able to stay part of the time) she will gain by mixing with other children. She will learn to share and is bound to widen her play experiences. She is likely to stay for dinner, which becomes a new social activity, and she will probably have a rest in the afternoon. So long as she enjoys the experience, it is excellent preparation for school.

Q Do you think it could be harmful for our small children to see us naked? What do you feel about parents and children bathing or taking a shower together? Several of our friends seem to allow their children into the bathroom with them.

Far from being harmful, it is natural that your children should see you naked. The one essential is that you ensure that the occasion is a natural one and that you do not appear embarrassed. Do not take your clothes off in front of the children because you feel you ought to.

Looked at from a child's point of view, it will not be odd that you see him without clothes when you bathe him. It would be odd if he had his clothes *on* when having a bath! In exactly the same way, he knows you don't wear clothes in the bath, so if you are not coy and don't shut him out of the bathroom and tell him not to come in, he will wander in without really noticing that you don't have any clothes on. Everything depends on his parents behaving naturally.

I am aware that some parents do not feel natural without clothes in the presence of their children. I just hope that you can get over the problem because it is not a problem for your children to start with, but could become one if you combine nudity with embarrassment.

Your feelings will inevitably depend on how you were brought up. If your parents made it very clear that you must never see them naked, you are bound to feel embarrassed. Talk the whole thing out with your husband or wife. Fortunately, today's parents are much more able to talk and behave naturally in this respect.

It will therefore be obvious from what I have said that it is perfectly natural for parents and children to bathe or have a shower together. And the same may go for swimming now that the opportunities have increased.

Having emphasized the natural aspect, I must point out that your children are very likely to comment on the differences between your bodies and theirs. Breasts, the penis, and pubic hair may be of particular interest to them. The most likely cause for embarrassment will be your husband's penis. A child with natural curiosity may want to touch it. This is not a sexual advance but a normal way of trying to learn more about a new strange object. If your husband can treat the whole occasion in a natural way and not show any embarrassment, the child will accept his explanation and soon move on to something else of interest that may have nothing at all to do with bodies.

There is no reason at all why children should not see their parents naked, providing they – the parents – do not feel embarrassed and the occasions are treated naturally. Be prepared, however, for comment on the differences between your bodies and theirs. This, too, is perfectly natural.

Q My husband has been out of work for a while now, but I have managed to find a job. Do you think it could harm our baby's development in any way if we swap roles for a while? It would certainly help in our present predicament.

In these days of high unemployment, such an anxiety is quite understandable but I don't think you will do your baby's development any harm at all by swapping roles. In fact, both your husband and your baby could gain enormously from such role reversal. Not only will they get to know each other better, but your husband should find his confidence in handling your infant increases tremendously. They will probably also have great fun together, so that instead of being depressed as a result of being out of work, your husband will enjoy himself and be contributing to the family's welfare in the bargain. You, in your turn, will feel fulfilled instead of depressed at seeing your husband just sitting about or arriving home with more job application failures to report. What is more, you will all gain from the income you are able to bring in.

I do think, however, that your husband would be wise to continue to look for a job when the opportunity arises. This will be good for his morale, for it is important that he does not forget that his primary role is that of breadwinner. Of course, I am aware that some families do a permanent swap of roles, but this has always seemed to me somewhat unnatural.

Don't keep your arrangement secret but use it to advantage. Many potential employers are likely to be impressed by the way your husband is coping with the situation and this might turn the tables in his favor.

Q Am I very wrong to regard one of our three daughters as my favorite?

Rather than being wrong as such, I think it could be hazardous to regard one of your three daughters as your favorite.

It is perfectly natural to find different aspects of personality and appearance attractive in our children. We love both "because" and "in spite of." But the very word "favorite" carries a much stronger connotation, and such feelings will most probably prevent you from judging your three children equally. Even if you think that she doesn't realize how you feel about her, though I suspect she probably does, you can be absolutely sure that the rest of your family is aware of your feelings so that an unfair situation may be created for the "favorite" because the others are likely to gang up on her. So for a myriad of reasons you must sort out your feelings and try to work out what has caused them.

The reasons for these feelings may be so deep that professional help is needed to bring them to the surface. One mother in labor, longing for a baby boy, heard the midwife call to her, "It's a girl!" She was so angry that she refused to handle the baby for three days. The next time she was in labor, she asked that no one should call out the sex. She took the new baby to her breast immediately after delivery, and it was a few minutes before she checked the sex: another girl. But, as she explained to me, this time she did not mind because the baby was already hers. Now she is aware she feels closer to the second baby and feels guilty that she doesn't love the first one in quite the same way.

Q Our four-year-old has announced that he is going to marry me when he grows up, which greatly amused both his father and me. Can you tell us if such an attachment is common at this age, or something to be concerned about? We wonder what could have put the idea in his head.

Your four-year-old has paid you the greatest compliment. You only offer marriage to the person you love most and he is indicating that this person is you.

He knows nothing of the nature of marriage, but is showing that he never wants to be parted from you. I am therefore sorry that you and your husband are amused by his statement of love, because if he realized you thought it funny, he would be deeply hurt.

You ask if such an attachment is common at his age and the answer is that it is, though very often a child will choose someone close to him other than his mother. Be flattered he has paid you the honor.

Q Do you think it is wrong to hit a child?

I think it is very wrong to hit a child because it brings him up to believe that punishment by assault is right. Consequently, he will use similar methods later on when he has children. I once met a father who had spent a total of eighteen years in prison for assault. It transpired that his father had whipped him regularly when he did wrong. I saw him because his seven-year-old son, whom he used to thrash, behaved so wildly that he had already been in police hands.

Hitting a child when he does something wrong doesn't teach him anything except the need to make sure he is not caught the next time. Moreover, the punishment—far from acting as a deterrent—makes the child feel he has paid for his misdeed. Children need explanations if they are to learn, not a thrashing.

One dangerous risk is that the parent who hits may be out of control so that he does serious damage to the child. An angry person is not going to take care that he doesn't strike too hard. Another serious sequel of hitting a child is that he may repeat the behavior towards other children. It is as though he has been licensed to hit, although he will probably choose children smaller than himself and thus become a bully.

Q **We are unable to have another baby and would like to extend our family by adopting another child. How can we best explain to five-year-old Lucy that she may soon have a baby sister or brother? Should we explain that the baby has been adopted?**

Your question does not suggest that you have already been promised a baby. Therefore, because there are so few babies available for adoption, I would not tell Lucy anything until you are sure that a baby has been allocated to you.

I imagine that by now you have told Lucy how a baby is made. This means that you must first explain that you and your husband are unable to have another baby even though you want one very badly.

Lucy will wonder why the new baby is going to be given away and, depending on the circumstances, you will need to explain that the baby's real mother, though she loves the baby very much, has not been able to look after the baby and therefore wants her to go to a loving home and be part of a family, just like Lucy is.

So much will depend on the questions Lucy asks, which you must answer with total truth. Much also depends on how much warning you get of the impending arrival of the new baby. Hopefully this will be a few weeks, but sadly it is often only a few days or even a few hours. It is for this reason that I am campaigning for adoptive parents to be told while the baby is still in the biological mother's uterus. If you have good warning, you and your husband will have time to make the necessary adjustments and to help Lucy understand all your preparations.

Lucy is old enough to understand the difference from a normal birth but she will need a lot of help to adjust. However, I am always amazed by the ability of children to make adjustments about all sorts of happenings, as long as they are told the truth and their questions answered so that they feel able to go on asking more.

Q **How important do you think it is that our three-year-old sees the babysitter before we leave for an evening out? Just occasionally, we find it difficult to time things so that the sitter arrives before he gets to sleep.**

I think it is very important that your three-year-old meets the babysitter before you leave to go out for the evening. It must be terrifying for a toddler to wake up in the night and find only a stranger in the house with him. I would therefore regard it as essential that the babysitter comes to meet your child on a previous occasion, if there is a risk that the sitter arrives after he has gone to sleep.

Alternatively, you will have to try to keep him awake until the babysitter arrives, and will just have to go out later than you had planned.

Talking of babysitters, one is bound to think of how to choose someone who is suitable. The most important thing is that the child should like the babysitter and vice versa. Having met beforehand, the babysitter should be briefed in all aspects of coping with any of the needs of the child, whether they be related to food, to toilet, or to any other essentials that are likely to arise while she is in charge.

I have written "she" but in fact some men make very good babysitters, and sometimes you can have an arrangement whereby a male student does babysitting as part of his rent. The prejudice against male babysitters is misplaced, and they are normally just as trustworthy as a female babysitter, if you choose correctly.

Be sure to leave a list of information that the sitter requires. He or she will need to know where you are and also the telephone number of the person whom she should call if she is unable immediately to make contact with you. It is usual to give the telephone number of the doctor, but I would far rather she made contact with you unless there is some very dire emergency. The babysitter needs to know where everything is and what your child's special words are for those objects that children call by different words.

Building sand castles may well turn out to be great fun, but bear in mind that certain aspects of a holiday environment may prove a little frightening at first to a toddler. Opinions vary as to whether parents should teach their children to read. But certainly it will be a good idea to encourage your child to look at books right from a very early age. A small child will usually benefit enormously, too, from learning to care for a pet.

One of the troubles with babysitters is that they are expensive. Therefore, if you can possibly arrange a scheme among a group of parents so that you share the babysitting, you will save money and also increase your circle of friends.

Q **What sort of vacations do you recommend for the under-fives? We are wondering what the children would enjoy best.**

I don't think the under-fives require a vacation in the sense of a change. They so enjoy their possessions and having a room of their own that they don't need a holiday in the same way that an adult does.

Adults need a vacation to get away from it all but for a child life should be the exact opposite. Home to a child should be such fun that he can't bear to leave it. That doesn't mean to say you shouldn't take young children on vacations. Moreover, children love the prospect of an adventure even if they hate leaving all their toys

behind which is why they always want to bring so many with them.

Adults want a vacation as a break from work whereas children, although not needing a vacation, can benefit enormously from a total change of scene and a whole new experience such as a trip to a farm or to a resort. But parents must be aware that farm animals are often frightening to a child the first time they meet a large one. Similarly, children can be very scared by big waves, and sand in your pants itches so a vacation near the sea is a mixed blessing for a child despite the excitement of sand castles and watching the tide come in and knock them down. The secret lies in viewing all these new experiences through your child's eyes and for father, in particular, to make the most of the opportunity of spending more time with his children.

Children under the age of five are not likely to fit easily into hotel life because parents are so liable to be forced into trying to achieve higher standards than at home because of the other hotel guests; this is very bewildering for young children. It is much wiser to rent your own accommodation and to feel free to be your normal

selves. This could be a cabin, a motor home or a tent. I was amazed at what an early age my own children took to camping.

Lastly, a vacation with children must mean putting their needs first. Don't exhaust them with sightseeing. If you have close friends with children of a similar age who get on well, you may find a joint vacation a great success.

Q Should we be teaching our four-year-old to read?

Opinions differ as to whether it is a good idea for parents to teach their children to read. Certainly, in the past most teachers were not in favor of parents taking on the role of teacher. The reason for this was that, not having been trained as teachers, they might use methods that were in conflict with those used in the school.

Of course, talking to a child is essential in order to encourage verbal communication, but the teaching of reading has traditionally been regarded by most teachers as *their* job.

Having said all this, there is now a move to

involve parents in teaching to a much greater extent, and I agree with this concept. Parents can be a wonderful extra source of help. Therefore, I hope that teachers will enlist the help of parents by telling them what they want them to do and, in a sense, use them as assistant teachers without losing the role of parent.

The whole subject is one that you must talk over with the teacher. I hope that you have a teacher who works and cooperates with parents to the extent that you are told what he or she would like you to do. This will mean that your child can be learning more. Parents are needed as partners to help teachers, and the modern concept is that teachers should be teaching parents how to be teachers' aides. In fact, it has been shown experimentally that where teacher and parent work together to help a child in his reading, the child may be a year or even two years ahead of those who do not have the advantage of this parent-teacher partnership.

Most children want to learn to read, just as they are excited by any new skill. The one essential is to handle them well so this new discovery is encouraged. Never make them feel they have to read or scold them if they are slow.

Q Is a five-year-old child too young for a pet?

The most suitable age for a child to have a pet varies enormously. He should be old enough to understand that a pet is a living animal requiring the same sort of care that he, himself, needs. It will also depend to great extent on the type of pet, since a goldfish will be safer from harm than a puppy or a kitten.

With these provisos, I think the best age is the youngest possible. Even two-year-olds may not be too young. Choose a pet that suits the whole family, even if one child is going to be the official owner. Having a living animal to love and to care for will teach your child many lessons. While he is at the stage when he is learning to control his own feelings, his pet will teach him that no one likes to be controlled all the time, although some control is essential for both pets and children.

A child needs to love as well as to be loved, and it helps to be able to lavish some of these feelings on his pet. He will also learn that his pet provides an outlet for some of his tensions. Best of all, when no one seems to understand him, he can rely on his dog, cat, or even his tadpole to remain loyal.

But don't make the mistake of putting your child totally in charge. He may not yet be old enough to accept total responsibility, and tragedies have resulted when a pet has not been fed because a child who has been scolded by the parent takes it out on the pet.

Training a pet to be clean and clearing up his mess are all lessons in living, but don't use them as occasions for lectures, otherwise your child may come to hate his pet and maybe hurt him when you are not looking.

There are safety aspects to consider, too. A cat net, for instance, is an important safety precaution if you have a baby who still sleeps in a bassinet or crib. Cats love sleeping on a baby's head, and this can be very dangerous.

Finally, consider beforehand what you will do if the pet dies. A mother once told me that she found her child's goldfish floating dead when she came down in the morning. Without a thought as to the best way to handle the situation, she put the dead fish in the dustbin and then went to tell her child. He was so angry with what she had done that he would not talk to her for three weeks.

Dead pets need funerals and this can be an important introduction to bereavement. On no account go straight out and buy a replacement. Every dead individual—pet or granny—must be mourned. Remember also that it is a normal aspect of curiosity for a child to wonder what his dead pet looks like two months or so after being buried. So don't be shocked if he talks about digging him up to have a look.

Q What sort of explanation do you think is sufficient for the three-year-old child who asks where he came from? Is he too young for any sort of sex education?

As with all children's questions, the answer should be simple, honest and accurate. You must also only answer the question asked. The answer to this first question is "from Mummy's tummy."

This is all he wants to know at that moment, since he needs time to think it over. Consequently, he may ask a second question immediately or not for several weeks.

This question is "How did I get out?" But many parents think the follow-up will be "How did I get in?" However, if you have your head stuck in a rabbit hole, you don't ask how you got there!

This second question should be answered in very simple language, depending on your child's ability to understand. Even though he is young, he will be able to accept without difficulty that mothers have a hole at the bottom of the tummy, closed by a door which opens when the baby is fully grown and ready to come out.

The third question "How did I get in?" probably will not be asked until he is about 8 to 10 years, or even older. At this stage, most children—having reached the stage of understanding sexual intercourse—go through a phase of utter bewilderment that their parents could have done *that*.

One of the advantages today is that there are a lot of books on the market which will help in your explanation and are illustrated in a way that a child can understand. You will be wisest to take him along to the shop with you, since you will then learn which book he finds most interesting and helpful.

Q **What do you feel is the ideal age gap between children? I have often heard it said to be about two years.**

I would like first to turn this question another way around, since I am so often asked by couples *when* they should have children. The answer to this is simple: when you want them. Having said that, very young and very old mothers are likely to run into more obstetric problems, as well as problems with the baby; eighteen to thirty years of age is the ideal biological age for having a baby.

As to the ideal age gap, this depends entirely on the parents' thoughts on what will suit them best. One mother may be able to cope with two very young children separated by only one or two years. Another needs a gap of five years in order to be able to give herself entirely and for as long as possible to the first child. I think children enjoy being close in age, and I suspect jealousy is less; but an older child, handled well, enjoys mothering his or her young brother or sister, an opportunity that occurs less often with smaller families.

Of course, if you want a large family, you will need to make the gap less than five years. Remember, too, that children don't always come when they are wanted, and fertility decreases with age—so don't leave it too long.

Q **Peter is three years old and an only child. I have just learned that I am pregnant. How should I tell him about the new baby? Is it too soon to tell him now?**

The first thing, in your excitement at the news, is not to tell him immediately that he is going to have a new brother or sister. It's a thrilling prospect for you, but may be rather bad news for the toddler who has been the only apple of your eye for three years.

Children get very bored with waiting, and seven or eight months is an almost incomprehensible length of time to a toddler. If he starts to notice your change in shape, then of course you should tell him, but the surprising fact is that not all children notice a pregnant woman's gradual increase in size because it is so slow. Body image is also not something with which they are as familiar as adults.

Telling early or late depends on the child, but it may be appropriate to leave telling until the last few weeks of your pregnancy. Then he can touch your tummy and, if he is lucky, feel the baby move. Be sure to explain what a newborn baby looks like. Introduce him to a friend's new baby, if you can, since otherwise he may expect a toddler just like himself to emerge.

The way in which your child first meets his new brother or sister is vital and must be planned. If your baby is to be born in a hospital, your son should visit as soon as possible, and your husband should tell the nurse or receptionist that this is his first visit. She should then come to you, while your visitors wait outside, so that you can finish breastfeeding, put the baby in the cot, and move it a little away from the bed. You will then have both arms free to greet your son on arrival. Don't be surprised if he seems very bewildered at seeing you in bed, especially if you are in a room with a lot of strangers.

Don't talk about the baby or point him out: it's far better to let him find the baby. He may choose not to do so on the first visit—a sure sign of how his nose has been put out of joint—but he may of course ask to see the baby right away. Either way, it is important to realize that he may not react in quite the manner you had hoped. Don't feel hurt if he doesn't welcome your baby in the loving way that you do.

Let him hold the baby if he wants to, and try not to keep telling him to take care. Babies are very resilient as long as they aren't dropped!

The days are coming when more children are being allowed to be present when the new baby is born, and many of the problems described above will fade away. It isn't long since the concept of fathers being present was thought indecent, and I now know of a number of children who have been thrilled to be present at the new brother or sister's birth.

Parents will naturally worry lest seeing a baby born will frighten their child, but children are so interested in anything new that their excitement overcomes any fears. Of course, if parents have doubts, they would be wise not to have the child present because he may sense their feeings and become alarmed, since anxiety is so contagious.

Understanding Behavior

Q **Our two-year-old son hates having his hair washed. Why does he protest so much? Can you suggest how we might make it more bearable for him in future?**

There must be few toddlers who have not hated having their hair washed at some time, so your two-year-old is in good company. But that doesn't make it any easier for you. I think the main problem is fear, whereas everything else about being bathed can be such fun.

If he has once had soap in his eyes, he won't forget it. Water in the eyes can be just as unpleasant. So don't go on trying to wash the soap out of his eyes when really it's the water you keep using that makes him cry. Wearing swimming goggles can make all the difference.

I suspect that fear of drowning can be part of the problem, so don't wash his hair in the bath when he's already surrounded by so much water and don't pour water onto his head. A damp face cloth is much less frightening and can be quite effective for wetting and rinsing.

Never allow hair-washing to end on an unhappy note. If it does, he will take much longer to get back his confidence. Let your child choose the shampoo and do the rubbing himself. Try to make it fun. Encourage him to make soap patterns in his hair and to look at the result in the mirror.

Some children are happy to have their hair washed under a shower, if you happen to have one. Others are prepared to sit with their backs to the sink so that they lean backwards rather than forwards, thereby keeping their faces uncovered.

If all these measures fail and hair-washing still brings tears, cut it out for a month. Merely keep his hair as clean and non-greasy as possible with a damp cloth. Battles can have such a lasting effect.

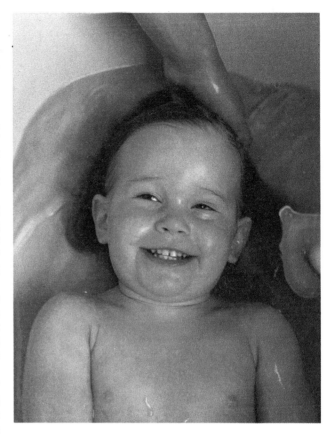

There are many ways to make shampooing fun, so that having her hair washed need in no way be traumatic for a child.

Q **How should I punish my child?**

Discipline has been well described as the way in which parents show their understanding of child development. The more experienced they become, the less they punish their children. This is because they have learned subtle methods of handling so that the child does what is wanted without the necessity of a direct command. Counseling of adults as a form of therapy is doomed to failure if it is directive. A nondirective approach is essential whether the behavior you are trying to alter is that of a child or an adult.

Of course, there are times when a direct approach to discipline is required, particularly in relation to safety. But this requires an explanation of dangers rather than the use of punishment. Parents should anticipate when a child will make the sort of mistakes that could lead to an accident. If the reason for the danger is explained, the response is much more likely to be successful.

The greatest mistake is to punish in anger. Lack of control is dangerous, and a blow could seriously harm the child. Moreover, it teaches the child nothing at all except to be more careful not to be found out next time. It also licenses him to strike others since he could not imagine that his parents would be so unfair as to use methods of behavior that were banned to him. He won't beat his parents, however; he will choose his small sister instead. By the way, I never cease to be staggered by the number of parents I meet who believe they are right to bite their child if they see him bite another one.

How, then, should you punish for some misdemeanor? Try to do so as infrequently as possible, by using more subtle techniques, and by avoiding a physical approach. The removal of privileges—such as forbidding a favorite TV program that day—may be effective. On no account should punishment be stored up. Immediate action is essential if punishment is absolutely necessary. The worst approach is to threaten a child with his father's homecoming.

Much of the way we handle the type of punishment we mete out relates to our own upbringing. Spanking in childhood breeds parents who spank and those from lower socioeconomic groups are more likely to use physical punishment than those in the professional classes. The wise parent forestalls trouble rather than punishing after the event. The worst trap to fall into is to threaten to punish and then to find the child has called your bluff, so that you either use brute force or land up in a battle of wits as to how to get out of your unfortunate threat.

Q **Do you think that sending a child to bed is a wise form of punishment? Could it be harmful in any way?**

Under no circumstances should a child be sent to bed as a punishment. Bed should be a child's castle at night. In it, he should feel safe and cozy, so that he has no fears about going to sleep when the appropriate time comes. It must not serve a dual function and be a "prison cell" in the daytime. What better way to make a child refuse to go to bed at night!

Moreover, what does any normal child do when sent to his room, let alone to bed, as a punishment? He begins to dislike the very place that he should feel as entirely his own.

I am always emphasizing how difficult life must, at times, seem to a child. This is a good example, since parents want their children to go to bed willingly, yet some are prepared to make it a punishment as well.

Q **Our four-year-old has picked up some awful words at play school. We are horrified to hear him speaking like this. How can we best discourage him from using this vocabulary?**

I suggest that you take no notice of him when he uses the offending words. I doubt if the real meaning of the words that horrify you make any technical sense to him. But he has discovered that he can get you into a state by using them. He is clearly enjoying this new-found power over you. It is as though he has hit the jackpot.

Scolding him and insisting that he does not say

the words will only make him use them more. Your biggest problem will be your relations and friends who must respect your request that they should take no notice. Hopefully, they will have had children, too, and be aware that you are handling him wisely.

Q **Our four-year-old keeps telling tall stories. What should we do to encourage him to tell the truth?**

Your four-year-old seems to be thoroughly enjoying himself and I suspect he is both imaginative and brighter than the average child of his age. He obviously enjoys both teasing you and having you on, just as lots of children do with their parents.

Treat the whole thing as a joke and be sure not to get irritated with him or tell him he's a liar. Play it all calmly instead of getting worked up and scolding him. There is no reason why you shouldn't join in the fun, too, by seeming to believe him and sometimes by telling *him* a tall story. When he goes to school the other children will decide how to handle him and he may need to readjust, but that won't be a great problem.

I would like to meet your son. He sounds very intelligent, with a delightful and well-developed sense of humor.

Q **Our four-year-old seems very accident-prone. Could there be something physically wrong?**

It is normal for children to have more accidents than adults, which is why you have to take extra care of them until they can look after themselves. But I don't like the use of the term "accident-prone" applied just to a child when it may in fact be the whole family that has brought this about.

Numerous studies have shown that it is the children who come from emotionally disturbed homes who are the ones to have more frequent accidents. For this reason, any doctor working in an accident department of a hospital knows he has to learn something about the family circumstances. Sadly, the child who has had one accident is much more likely to be the one to come back with another.

You will be aware that if you are upset, you don't drive your car as well and are therefore more liable to have an accident. The same goes for children; they don't take the proper precautions when they are upset or angry.

Some parents are so protective that they don't teach their children to protect themselves. If every time a child goes downstairs he is told to be careful, he never learns to cope alone. Always being told to take care actually prevents you from learning how to take practical precautions. We all learn from our minor mistakes unless someone is fussing about us.

You ask if there could be something physically wrong. There could be, but it is unlikely. The cause is far more likely to lie in the area I have described, but it is true that if there is a problem with his physical coordination for some reason, he would fall over more often. Some children are more clumsy than the average and they do have more accidents, but look at the way you are handling him before you ascribe the problem to a physical cause.

Q **Since the arrival of our baby, our two-year-old daughter has started to wet her pants, having been dry for quite some time now. As we imagine that the things must be related, what can we do to sort this problem out?**

I often think it must be awfully difficult to be a child and that, for this reason, we should always try to see problems through a child's eyes. The solution often comes more easily then. Just imagine what it must feel like to be an only child and one day to find that your parents have acquired another child—a baby, at that—who has more time spent on him than you get.

This makes the preparation for and introduction of the new baby so important. Explaining that you are going to have a new baby is vital, but never do this too early because children get bored and a nine months' wait is a very long time. Let your first child feel your tummy—she might be lucky enough to feel the baby move.

Meeting the baby for the first time must also be planned very carefully because seeing a new brother or sister intimately sucking at the breast can be very traumatic for a toddler. Of course, it will be particularly disturbing, too, if an older child is not allowed to visit you and the baby in the hospital, and this is something to check on when choosing a hospital. If a first introduction is postponed until the mother comes home, a child is liable to feel that her mother went away because she wanted someone nicer.

If any of these factors apply to the way in which your child was introduced to the baby, you can understand why she feels as she does. This understanding may also help for the next time. I am sure you are right that your daughter's wetting is connected to the new baby's arrival. You also

got her dry at quite a young age, so she is bound to relapse more easily than someone older.

Your main role now is to give her back the confidence that has been severely shaken by the arrival of the baby. Spend as much time as possible with her and pay as little attention as possible to the new baby, although this will not be easy. If she will let you, involve her in changing, feeding, and bathing the baby, as well as playing with him. Then your problems are almost over. Your first goal has to be to get her to accept and enjoy the new baby, rather than getting her dry. Remember, too, that she will be muddled by your making no complaint about the baby wetting the diapers, so don't be in a hurry to grumble at her wet pants.

It is likely that a major factor in her wetting is that she is trying to be like the baby who, unfairly in her eyes, is allowed to wet her diapers and is such a favorite of yours. Consequently, the worst thing you could do would be to put her back in diapers. Your task is to help her understand that, because she is more grown up, she has been clever and learned how to be dry.

Q **I should like to have our next baby at home. Do you think this would be a disturbing experience for our three-year-old son? We are concerned as to how he may react to the event.**

I think this is more likely to be a wonderful experience for your three-year-old. All babies used to be born at home so that their older brothers and sisters had a much more realistic understanding of birth even though they were not in the room at the time.

Having said that, in some homes children were actually present at the birth simply because there was nowhere else for them to go, but their presence had probably not been planned.

Your question does not give the impression that you are asking whether your three-year-old could witness the birth, but it is something to consider.

Some parents are now allowing their children to be present and a short while ago a mother of a four-and-a-half-year-old boy wrote to me to tell of her experience. She and her husband had the agreement of the hospital that their child could be present. He behaved perfectly and she described a point during the second stage of labor when she was getting tired and a pupil midwife threatened her with forceps if she did not push harder. Her son climbed onto the stool he had been given to make watching easier and suddenly shouted,

"He's coming, Mommy. I can see his black hair."

This was a crucial moment for the mother who wrote that her child talked as though he had delivered hundreds of babies. This caused her to relax and the baby, a girl, was born with the next contraction. What a wonderful family experience!

I am not suggesting that this should be universal, but rather that parents should consider the possibility since many children would gain enormously by the experience. Of course, the child should be carefully prepared and the parents would have decided he would not be frightened.

The longer I work with children, the more I am made aware that they will mostly accept any new experience provided they are not alone and provided the accompanying adults are not scared.

Q Our four-year-old still insists on joining us in bed in the middle of the night. It really disturbs our rest. We also feel he is too old to be acting this way. How can we best put a stop to it?

The best way to help you will be to explain the reasons lying behind this common problem. By a clearer understanding of your child's feelings, you will be better able to work out how to meet his needs so that he no longer has to come into your bed every night.

If a four-year-old still needs to come into your bed, the chances are that he simply does not feel safe on his own. No one should deny a baby the right to be in his mother's bed. Consider how the mothers of other animal species provide comfort and curl up around their young. Unfortunately, however, the supposed risk of "overlying" once stopped thousands of mothers from doing what they felt was natural, when in fact there was no danger at all, unless the mother had been sedated or had taken alcohol or drugs. Those mothers who did have their babies in bed with them, meanwhile, were made to feel guilty and subjected to almost intolerable warnings from well-meaning friends and relatives. Fortunately, a large group of mothers now trust their own instincts and have happily had their babies in bed with them, to the enormous benefit of both the babies and the parents.

I suspect that your four-year-old was not allowed in your bed at the beginning and perhaps, worse still, was put in a room of his own right from the start. This reverses the normal process whereby independence develops. If a baby is allowed to be an infant and to be dependent on his parents when he is newborn, the security this gradually engenders makes him want to grow up and to be independent. Consequently, when he is two or three years old, and often before then, he will happily settle in his own bed and relish having his own bedroom, especially if he has been allowed to choose the colors, and maybe even to help in the painting.

A child handled in this normal way will often be perfectly happy when very young to start the night in his own bed in his parents' room, knowing that he can climb into their bed when he feels lonely and that he will not be thrown out. A mother once told me that her six-year-old boy who, as a baby, had slept in his parents' bed, now was happy in his own room, except that on occasions he would come into his parents' bed in the middle of the night explaining, "Mom, I was having a loner."

The four-year-old who was denied this approach must now be allowed the baby stage that he missed when an infant. The best approach will vary from one child to another. One child will be made to feel safe by starting the night in his parents' bed and will come to accept that he is moved out when they come up to bed. Another will be helped towards a feeling of security by being allowed to stay downstairs with his parents, often going to sleep on the floor or couch, and then being taken to his own room when they go to bed. It's the business of being sent up to bed on your own that can be so frightening, especially if accompanied by those stupid words "go to sleep." Who can go to sleep when tense and frightened?

The child who cries out from his bed can be

Trying to bring the shy child out of his shell will inevitably require a great deal of sensitivity. You, as his parents, are the people most likely to be aware of his needs and the best tactics to use. But bear in mind, above all, that it is not a good idea to force a small child into situations that have proved frightening in the past. Gaining confidence is a gradual process.

quickly comforted by being tucked up and given a kiss, but this should not be drawn out. The essence is to help the child feel safe and to show that you care but on to account to allow him to bribe you so that you quite literally have your head on his pillow until he goes to sleep. He is bound to wake when you go! Equally, a child should never be left to cry since this will only increase the intensity of his fear and lengthen the time before he feels safe on his own.

Q **Our child seems to be hyperactive and is constantly restless and on the go. Nothing we do seems to calm him down. Why might that be?**

The word "hyperactive" has come into fashion during the last few years and has caused a great deal of unnecessary anxiety. Merely a descriptive term for a child who is more active than normal, it is not a diagnosis. Unfortunately, it has entered the field of jargon so that doctors as well as parents, teachers, and others use the term "hyperactivity" as though referring to one clear-cut condition, which is certainly not the case.

The commonest reason for a child being described as "hyperactive" is that he is naturally boisterous and that his high spirits are more than his parents can take. This is especially true if his parents fail to understand his needs and continually tell him to keep still or to be quiet.

The more they tell him to stop, the more he tests them out to see how far he can go before they explode. This is all part of the natural negativistic tendencies of the toddler. Keep a "no" chart for a few days and record a cross every time you give him a negative command. You will

probably be surprised by the number of crosses that appear.

Hyperactivity, it is claimed by some researchers, can sometimes be the result of certain additives and coloring matters in food. I am sure that some children have quietened down when placed on a special diet, but I am not yet convinced that it is the diet that caused the change. A detailed scientific trial between two comparable groups of children is needed to prove such a theory.

I have never prescribed a diet. I use behavioral methods of treatment, so that I work out with the parents and the child the reason for difficult behavior. From there, we make a plan of action, and I am constantly amazed by the speed with which children respond. This is because they do not actually enjoy being difficult but want to please their parents. Consequently, if parents work on the principle of praise for good behavior and take no notice of bad behavior, the child responds to the advantages gained by his good behavior.

Two other groups of very active children should be mentioned. Backward children, because they are less able to control themselves, may respond in this way. Secondly, certain drugs, especially phenobarbitone given for convulsions, may suppress a child's inhibitions and self control so that he becomes "hyperactive."

Q **Our three-year-old is unbelievably shy. How can we help him over this difficulty before he starts school next year?**

Children's temperaments are so variable that some are bound to be shy. The important aspect in handling your child is to respect his feelings, not to adopt a hearty and unsympathetic approach that would only force him still further into his shell.

You are going to have to work much more subtly and with greater sensitivity than with a noisy extravert. But this test of your skills is going to be fun, as long as you accept that it is only by your sustained efforts that he will acquire the confidence to overcome the insecurity he feels now. He might be helped by having a friend over to play, but on the other hand this might make him more shy. You, as parents, are the ones to work out his needs and the best tactics to use in order to help him. Suggestions from outsiders are so often wrong.

There is likely to be a very sound reason for his behavior. During early life, his need to be understood may not have been fully appreciated. Children who have to make big changes in their lives are likely to be more shy, so that moving can sometimes have a profound effect. This shows at its greatest in children who are adopted late. The fact that you, his parents, are constantly with him will help more than anything. On no account force him to play with others or to take part in activities that he has refused. It is probable that he is frightened of the game and you will have to work gently so as to give him confidence.

Q **How can we prevent the embarrassment of our three-year-old son constantly handling himself?**

First of all, it is important to be clear that it's only *you* who is embarrassed. What has probably happened is that you have at some time in the past drawn attention to this natural action of his, instead of distracting him. All children—both boys and girls—get extra pleasure from touching certain parts of their bodies, especially the genitalia. The action is reinforced by scolding, simply because it is forbidden.

Some of our grandparents believed that the child who masturbated might grow up to be a sex maniac or might go crazy or blind. In the last century, some boys were made to wear a metal cage so that playing with the genitalia became impossible. Modern parents have lost these fears but the old beliefs still influence the way some people think. I must therefore emphasize that the child will come to no harm.

Having walked into this problem, your job is now to show total lack of interest and never to scold him. Instead, try very subtly to interest him in something else, but if that fails walk out of the room so that you are not upset. Do everything you can, too, to prevent him from

reaching the stage of feeling guilty because that may only drive the habit underground.

You are bound to feel embarrassed if he masturbates in company. This will become less if you can talk about your feelings rather than acting as if you consider his behavior to be socially acceptable. Under these circumstances, as opposed to when you are alone with him, you may have to ask him to leave the room if he must go on behaving that way, but try distraction first.

Q **Our five-year-old refuses breakfast before leaving for school. Is this something to be concerned about? I don't like him to leave on an empty stomach.**

I am assuming that your five-year-old is perfectly well. In that case, I would not be concerned by his not eating breakfast. I would be very interested to know whether *you* eat a big hearty breakfast because I suspect that most adults eat very little breakfast except on holidays!

I must admit that, if I am staying in a hotel, I have a full breakfast and thoroughly enjoy it. But at home I have only orange juice and coffee. My wife has only coffee. I find I have a lot of friends with a similar pattern.

It does not matter *when* an individual eats during the day provided the total is adequate. You will know the answer to that with your child by whether he is energetic. Energy is the best sign that the body has enough food for growth and for energy.

Many people eat more than necessary and become fat in consequence. One of the great advances in child health is the appreciation that children can get too fat and as a result may need to have their calorie intake restricted. There was a time when it was solemnly believed that you couldn't put a child on a diet. Today we know that fat children often make fat adults.

Of course, school plays a part in what your child has for breakfast. If he comes down late, you may find yourself shouting to him to get off to school before he has even sat down. I am not suggesting you will alter this pattern, but try to imagine what his stomach must feel like.

One of the concerns of some mothers is that a child must have something warm inside him before he goes to school. I wish I knew the origin of this illogical belief. Food that is eaten cold must soon become warm as the temperature rises to body heat, whereas hot food will become cooler!

To those mothers who complain that their children don't eat anything before going to school, I ask if they always fill their car with gas in their garage before driving off! We are perfectly content to fill our cars during the day when they get low in gas, and I believe we should adopt the same approach towards our children who will certainly demand food when they feel hungry.

Q **Our three-year-old boy keeps nagging us to buy him a doll. Could there be any harm in this? Is it normal for a boy to want to play with dolls? What do you suggest we do?**

Your small son's request is perfectly natural. Why shouldn't he enjoy playing with little people and looking after them, just like his sister? After all, we have male nurses as well as female ones!

The whole problem stems from the parental fear that the boy who likes dolls is going to turn out to be effeminate, or perhaps even a homosexual.

If parents can understand that this is just one more variety of a normal child's play, involving an imaginative and caring approach to people, it will be seen by them in quite a different light.

Playing with dolls is another opportunity for brothers and sister to play together, though the child acting as mother may be so possessive of her "children" that she won't share them with anyone. Her concept of parenthood at this age is not one of sharing.

Fortunately for all concerned, toymakers have saved the situation by producing various strongly male figures. Fathers are not worried when their sons play with these "dolls," and I have been able to remove the anxiety from many distressed parents by recommending they purchase one of them.

A particularly interesting point is that I have no recollection of parents coming to see me because their little girls wants to play with soldiers.

Q **Our four-year-old seems to have been having a lot of bad dreams lately. What might be causing them?**

A child relives in his dreams some of his daytime activities. If these have been very exciting, and especially if they were frightening, they will give him bad dreams.

Obviously, you can't protect him from ever being frightened, nor would it be a natural life for him if you did so, but you can make sure that comfort is immediately at hand both by way of a warm cuddle and sympathy. Children who feel safe are much less liable to be frightened and will get

over the episode more quickly. Never suggest to your child that she is being babyish and should be more brave. This will only make her less confident. Try another approach. Praise her for her bravery whenever the opportunity arises. (I hope your husband gives you and your daughter comfort, too, when you or she are feeling miserable or frightened.)

Children are more likely to have bad dreams if they are not given a chance to switch off from some violent or exciting activity before going to bed. The bedtime story is of the utmost importance in this respect, and provides a cozy time for parents as well. This may be the only time that Daddy has with them during the weekdays. He is also likely to feel flattered by their waiting up for their father to read to them. It will bring him home earlier, too!

The one essential when your child cries out with a bad dream is to go to her immediately and offer comfort. I hope you would never leave her to cry or just tell her to "shut up."

Q **Mealtimes are becoming intolerable. Our toddler simply refuses to eat, whatever I have prepared. What can we do about it?**

I suspect that by now you are actually showing your toddler that you are very concerned that he should eat. In consequence, having found your vulnerable area, he enjoys playing on it. This is one variety of negativistic behavior. (Refusal to have bowels open or to speak are others.)

A toddler will commonly react in this negative fashion to the area of behavior in which he is most pressurized.

What is more, and perhaps not unexpected, the particular pressure area adopted by a parent is likely to be the same as that adopted by his or her own mother a generation ago. I was once asked to see a child who would not eat. Most of all, he rejected the peas that his mother would hide in the mashed potatoes. I later discovered that the mother, as a child, had been faced with exactly the same behavior from *her* mother but had entirely forgotten about it. Her brain, like a computer, had somehow been set to be concerned about peas.

The best way around the problem is to take all pressure off your toddler in the field of eating. Rather than saying "eat up," simply make it clear that at the end of the meal you will remove his plate whether he has eaten or not. This is not a punishment but a way of life to which he will gradually respond. Never make him sit over meals, but make mealtimes as easy and enjoyable as

possible. Choose the foods he likes best and don't be afraid to repeat the same meal fairly often. Children are very conservative in their likes and dislikes as far as food is concerned.

In time, having made the helpings small so that it will be easy for him to finish his plate, you'll probably find him asking for more before you know where you are.

Q **Is four-year-old Michael unusual in carrying his blanket everywhere with him?**

I think the most accurate and direct answer is to

say that your son's behavior may seem unusual but a lot of children do still cling to a comforter of some kind at that age. In fact, I suspect that if a young child gets really hooked on a blanket or other transitional object, he is likely to hang on to it for years, although hopefully he will increasingly forget to pick it up as other activities take his interest and security arrives from other sources.

Often a rag or a piece of blanket, or perhaps a muslin type of diaper is carried around everywhere by the child, usually with one end of it in his mouth. It would be interesting to analyze where the process starts. I am sure that some children, whenever they are feeling lonely in bed, chew a bit of a sheet for comfort. The process then becomes fixed so that the

child finds a smaller cloth for daytime use whenever he is in need of comfort.

I do not recollect any parents telling me they gave the child a blanket, rather that he acquired it by himself. But I expect there are a few exceptions to this.

There is no doubt that smell adds to the comfort given by the blanket. Indeed, many parents will have been faced with an irate toddler complaining vociferously that it's no good now and doesn't smell the same when it has been washed while he was asleep.

Weaning the child from his blanket is very difficult and requires the utmost subtlety. The child's attachment to the blanket is intense, and switching his interest to something else is very difficult. You may need to "lose" it during the night but this will certainly mean displays of wrath and howling for a time.

You must also ask yourself if it does him any harm because you can be sure that the teasing when he reaches school will make him drop the habit there, although it may continue at home.

Many parents, for sound reasons, are concerned by the effect of the blanket on the erupting teeth. The answer is the same as for thumb-sucking. Only if the habit continues into the second dentition, which starts to appear at around six years, is there any

danger of affecting the position of the teeth. Before then, the gums are fortunately not affected so that the permanent teeth come through in the correct position.

Q Our three-year-old daughter had a very bad tantrum in a store recently and nothing seemed to get through to her. How should we best handle such a display if it ever happens again? What can we do to prevent a tantrum?

Your child may be on the way to becoming what I call a "supermarket child." She has learned how to embarrass you when you are at your most vulnerable. The direct answer to your question is that you should not take her shopping until you are sure you are over the problem so that she will not use this very strong weapon against you again.

But most important is to prevent things reaching this stage. In other words, how do you prevent temper tantrums, whenever they occur? No one likes performing to an empty stage, so I advise you to get out of the room as fast as you can once you see a tantrum developing. On no account shut the door, which is an aggressive act, and which may lead a child to kick it. Leave it open, and make a noise so she knows where you are. One way would be to dash to the kitchen, shouting how you left the saucepan on the stove. *Your* behavior will provide such a shock that it will probably distract her.

If you are successful, the tantrum will not develop, but if it does, leave her to kick on the floor until she quietens enough for her to allow you to pick her up and comfort her. If you pick her up at the height of a tantrum, she may only kick you and prolong the outburst.

If you use these tricks correctly, you will stop the tantrum developing any further. If, however, you have indeed reached the "supermarket child" stage, make it plain that you are not going shopping again with her until her conduct at home and elsewhere has shown you that you can trust her not to behave in this way.

Q Our four-year-old son is extremely bright for his age and we feel that he may be particularly gifted. He is constantly asking us very complex questions. Would it be worthwhile taking him for any special intelligence tests?

It is important to know, of course, in what way your child appears bright. I think that many four-year-olds of ordinary intelligence are thought to be unusually bright when really they are simply behaving normally for their age, and asking a lot of questions. The age of four is also to an extent the time when a young child is likely to emerge from the battles of the negativistic age.

As long as his parents are understanding, all the many questions that a child will naturally ask will be answered by them. It is to be hoped, too, that he will not be scolded for asking so many questions. I sometimes feel very sad when it is apparent that parents have become tired of their child's questions and that they have been trying to get him to shut up. I would hope that parents would regard questions as one of the very important aspects of childhood because they are so relevant to the whole learning process.

Very possibly, your child is unusually gifted, but I am wondering why you want to have him tested for this. There seem to be no indications of behavioral problems, so presumably you want him tested for your own information and possibly for your own pride. I would accept him for what he is, and continue to encourage him in the normal way. If you have him tested and find that he is

not above average, you are bound to be disappointed and you might start to handle him differently.

With regard to the special intelligence tests used to determine the intelligence quotient or I.Q, your child is really too young for this to be undertaken since the results are unlikely to be accurate. Most psychologists would not wish to test a child younger than five in this way, and would prefer that he had reached seven years of age.

Q Our two-year-old recently had a breath-holding attack during a tantrum. It was terrifying. What is the best way to handle such behavior? Is it in fact dangerous? Is there anything we can do to prevent it happening again?

I can understand your terror, having heard so many parents describing the same feelings. A breath-holding attack is best thought of as a very severe temper tantrum. The children who have them are usually those whose degree of frustration is greater than the average so that a fall or the removal of a toy by another child is enough to set it off.

The child is usually of toddler age, like yours, and has not yet learned to control his feelings. He has an attack only when someone important, usually his mother, is present. This is why doctors rarely see breath-holding as such. I have actually witnessed only two instances in my life, but I have seen hundreds and hundreds of children who have had such attacks.

The fact that there is an audience is essential— no one likes playing to an empty theater. This means that if only the mother can find a reason to dash out of the room when the first signs show, she may forestall the attack. Shout out that you forgot the cooking on the stove and fly to the kitchen. But be sure to leave the door open so he can follow you if he feels like it. You may notice how a fall alone in the yard never starts off an attack. It will only occur if you are there.

Fortunately the attacks are not dangerous in the sense of there being a risk that the child will die. I have never heard of a fatal breath-holding attack. But if you can't prevent one, you certainly want to stop an attack as soon as you can.

You have probably tried slapping his face or throwing cold water at him and found these methods to be ineffectual. Some mothers tell me they can stop an attack by blowing hard on the child's face. The best method I know, taught to me by a mother many years ago, is to put a finger in the child's mouth and to hook it over the back of the tongue so that you then draw the tongue forwards with your finger. This causes a reflex breath and one breath brings the attack to an end. Be sure to put your finger in as soon as possible while the mouth is wide open. The good thing is that older children don't get breath-holding attacks, though they show their tempers in other ways!

Q **Do you think I am right to refuse to let our small son have a toy gun? He keeps asking for one.**

I do not like to encourage aggression any more than you do, but if you deny your child such a toy you will almost certainly reinforce his desire for one.

Every normal boy goes through a phase of "shooting" people. This normally starts with a stick, so your denying him a toy gun won't help at all. "Bang, bang, you're dead!" is the normal battle cry of all young children. A problem only arises if *parents* take the words literally and develop a hang-up that bewilders the child. To a toddler, the word "dead" merely means "get out of my way" and is totally reversible in his young mind.

Boys enjoy playing with guns more than girls do and it probably helps them learn how to control their natural aggression. There is also an element of imitation since guns feature so much on television. It takes time for a child's understanding of games to catch up with reality but you will be wise to explore this aspect when he's old enough to understand.

Q **Our daughter is repeatedly teased at playschool because of her port wine stain birthmark. What should we do to help her through this? Can it be covered up?**

A "port wine stain" causes a mauve skin area and, although often seen, is not the most common variety of birthmark. The commonest—a strawberry mark—is likely to have faded or at least to have begun to fade by the time a child goes to school.

Port wine stains and strawberry marks are varieties of nevi that occur anywhere on the body. This means they are composed of immature and very small blood vessels called capillaries. Whereas strawberry marks disappear on their own after a few months, port wine marks persist. Ideally, therefore, these are removed surgically, but most of them are too big, in which case a special matching camouflage cream is used. The original was called "Cover – mark" but now most of the major cosmetic firms make a similar cream. This can be ordered by a dermatologist and he or she will tell you where to take your daughter for a technician to prepare a cream that matches her skin. Similar creams can be made for boys, and all are of a pancake-base variety.

I once saw a girl of about eight years old who, when she was teased, would beat up the offending child! Result: she was suspended from school. Once she had her camouflage cream, she was no longer teased and the school problem ceased.

One last point related to the site of port wine stains: a mauve mark is commonly present at the top end of the cleft between the buttocks in certain ethnic groups. These are those of black, Oriental or Mediterranean origin. It is called a Mongolian blue spot after the Mongol race and has nothing to do with Down's Syndrome (mongol) babies. This racial mark usually fades as the child gets older.

Q **Our babysitter found our four-year-old banging his head against the wall on purpose. This is obviously very worrying to us.**

Your babysitter is very wise to have told you about what she has seen because head-banging is serious. Sadly, even today, we read about it being a common habit and that a child will "grow out of it." That is nonsense. Maybe he will, but the all-important fact is that it is an indication of problems that need dealing with now.

It is not always easy to stop the actual head-banging, but your aim must be to distract him so that he moves to some new and interesting game. Best of all, be on the look-out for the early signs that he is beginning a bout of head-banging in order to get him onto another activity before the bout begins.

Obviously, it is abnormal for a child to hurt himself in order to draw attention to his needs, and yet that is exactly what is happening. Something has occurred for your child no longer to be able to find pleasure in the ordinary ways of life. He feels so miserable and bored with life that his mood sometimes makes him hurt himself as the only way of finding solace and pleasure. He is depressed and unhappy. Whatever is underlying these feelings must be worked out and put right. In trying to discover what is wrong, the approach needs to be that of a detective, and very possibly the help of a pediatrician will be

needed. For this sort of situation, it is the child's relationship with his mother that is the likely one to have become disturbed. He needs to be cuddled and shown affection in a physical way.

Just spending lots of extra time with him and being demonstrative may bring about a change in behavior, even though you can't pinpoint the exact cause. But if this doesn't work and he is still unhappy, be sure to seek medical help. Having emphasized the serious underlying emotional reasons for head-banging, I must make it clear that it does not cause brain damage, the frequent fear held by parents.

Q Every time our normally helpful four-year-old comes back from nursery school he is extremely uncooperative and bad-tempered. What can the reason be for this?

There is no quick answer to your important question but clearly something is upsetting him badly. It would be interesting to know what he says when you ask him what is wrong. But probably, if he even answers, he simply says he doesn't know.

Your question suggests that he is happy at his nursery school and no doubt you have asked his teacher how he behaves there. I presume that he has settled into the school and isn't being bullied.

Possibly he likes school very much and enjoys all the creative play, finding home very different. One problem could be that the time he comes home is also an especially busy time for you, as his mother, so that he gets left on his own. It could be that, in his own way, he is telling you he isn't all that happy about coming home and finding he gets insufficient attention. So you are absolutely right to be trying to find out what these displays of mood are all about.

He wants to please you but every now and then things go wrong and he is scolded. The basic principle for success is to praise his good behavior and to disregard the bad. Sadly, it often happens that the reverse occurs so that no notice is taken of the time when the child is

Far left Visiting the nursery school or playgroup with your child before leaving him or her there alone should help to dispel unnecessary fears, just as instilling confidence by very practical means such as a night light or bedroom door left ajar will help the child who is scared of the dark.

playing on his own, whereas when he is naughty he does get attention. Being left alone can be so distressing to a child that he does something wrong simply in order to get your attention, even if it brings a scolding or punishment with it.

I also suggest you keep a "no" chart. Mark a cross on a sheet of paper you keep prominently in the kitchen every time you tell your child not to do something. You may be surprised at how often you correct him!

It would be ideal if his father played with him as soon as he came home, while you prepare the supper or put the baby to bed. This way your child will look forward to his father's return, and father will have a special time to enjoy, as well as an opportunity to get to know his son better.

It is essential to find out the reason for your child's unhappiness. If the answer fails to come to light from the suggestions I have made, you should talk to your doctor. A good doctor will work like a detective, placing all the bits together and gradually working back until he finds what is at the root of the problem and thereby a solution.

Q **Our four-year-old son is absolutely terrified of the dark. How can we best encourage him to be more confident at night? What bedtime procedures should we adopt? Should we let him come into our room whenever he feels frightened? Or is it better to insist that he braves the dark?**

Fear of the dark is common and is usually started by some frightening incident. On no account should the child be made to feel stupid or babyish. I am sure there are some things that frighten you—heights perhaps. Nor must he be made to feel he has to be brave and not show or talk about his fear. It's rather like telling someone to stand up for himself. In World War I, soldiers were shot for being frightened and running away—hardly the ideal therapy for such fear, often found in very brave men who had temporarily come to the end of all they could tolerate.

The basic approach to the handling of such a fear

in young children is to do something practical to make it less frightening. A night light will get rid of the dark, and leaving the bedroom door open may also make a child feel safer. You don't get rid of natural fears by being forced to face them, but by being helped to see that fears can be reduced by simple means.

Tell your child that he can come into your room if he is very frightened. Knowing that this is allowed makes all the difference and prevents a child from lying awake terrified, too frightened to move. Loneliness in the dark is especially frightening.

Q Why does our baby seem to enjoy dropping things on purpose so much?

Your baby, at about eight months old, has made the exciting discovery that when you drop things they don't disappear forever. Until now, a toy that he has thrown out of the stroller or off the table disappeared and was forgotten. Then came the great day, at about this age, when he reached the stage at which he was able to follow the object down to the ground. This was a red letter day for him—and, I hope, for you as well.

Having understood that his toy is on the floor, he will very rapidly try to get you to pick it up. Naturally, he will then drop it again because, perhaps for the first time, he has learned how to get you to do what he wants. The only trouble is that you will get bored before he does, and he would certainly go on dropping the toy all day for you to pick up, if you were to let him.

Sadly this particular game nearly always ends with a mother getting irritated and telling her child to stop dropping the toy. How very strange her reactions must seem to the child who one moment has his mother enjoying his game and, the next, angry with him for playing in exactly the same way with her.

Of course, what the mother should do is to change the game when she gets bored. She does not have to pick up the toy and she can easily start to interest him in something else. Perhaps it is time to do some cooking, so she can move him with her to the kitchen and give him a large plastic bowl and wooden spoon to stir the pudding he is making.

I always suggest that parents should keep a baby book for recording important milestones of development like this one, rather than boring details such as weight. When a child is older, and especially when he or she has children, this book will be invaluable. In fact, if the book is also illustrated with photographs, you will probably find it is your children's most popular book—it was with mine.

Q Maria—she's three—is unbelievably jealous of the new baby. Candidly, she has even exhibited violence. How can we handle this? My wife is too frightened to leave them alone together even for a moment. Do you think that it could really be dangerous?

You have given a vivid description of the situation facing many parents, and your wife is right to be so frightened as not to leave them alone because of the risk that your older child will harm the baby.

My first emphasis is therefore to underline the need for the steps you must take to reduce this risk. You will be aware that this intense jealousy has resulted from the shock the older child received when she realized that you had a new baby. She may even have felt that this was to replace her. Certainly, she no longer feels safe, and to her the only solution is to get rid of the new baby. Attempted murder is not too strong a term for the actions that parents have described to me. One toddler was very nearly successful in smothering the baby with a pillow when the parents arrived in the nick of time. Another jealous child filled the new baby's mouth with stones, so that he was black in the face and choking when his parents found him.

Understanding the cause of your older child's intense feelings will help you work out the right solution. The first thing is on no account to scold her, although this is bound to be your first reaction. Scolding her may only make matters worse because she may plan some action in which she takes care not to be found out. She has to be helped to understand the reasons for her very normal feelings and why she is so angry with you for getting a new baby. Just imagine what it must feel like for an only and much loved child suddenly to discover, without warning, that she has a rival in the form of a new brother or sister.

You may have tried to explain this to her, but the important point is that she did not understand what you were saying. I feel it is unlikely that you took sufficient steps to reduce this risk of jealousy.

Hopefully, she will come to understand some of the reasons for her feelings. Go over it all very slowly, making it quite clear that you do know how she feels and emphasizing that she is not to blame but that it is your fault for not explaining things properly beforehand.

The next step is to give her almost all your attention. Feeding and changing the new baby are activities you should share with her. Her reaction won't change until you make her feel safe again in your love. Obviously, you won't leave her with the baby until the problem is over. Exposing her less often to periods of potential jealousy will also help.

Do things on your own with Maria, and when your husband comes home from work make sure he goes straight to her. It would probably help if he made no comment about nor any active move towards the baby.

You are bound to be feeling that these recommendations are going to be harsh on the baby. Maybe they are, but remember we are dealing with potential risk. The baby will come to no long-term harm because he cannot appreciate what is happening, and you will still be the warm mother who cuddles and feeds him. Maria will also soon enjoy the extra attention instead of the scoldings she probably received before.

Bear in mind, too, that a dog can also become very jealous of a new baby if he has been very attached to you and has had a lot of individual attention. Think hard before you consider having a dog around with a baby in the house. A great deal of trust is required.

Q **Our baby starts screaming his head off as soon as we put him in the playpen. Why is that?**

The direct answer to your question is that he screams because he hates the playpen. I must admit that I don't blame him, and I regard the use of playpens as being very limited, and limiting.

In times of old, the playpen was used as a dumping ground where the child was supposed to occupy himself while the mother got on with her work. I hardly think it should have been called a "play" pen, rather just a "pen," because that is how so many children see it and is, I believe, the reason why your baby screams.

Since he screams because he hates the pen, it is up to you to work out why he hates it so. Is there some toy in the playpen that frightens him? The reason may of course also lie in his being aware that, once he has been put in the pen, he is left on his own, whereas he really wants to play.

One time a playpen is valuable is when your young toddler is with you in the kitchen and you are frightened that he may get hold of any of the dangerous utensils that you have there. In that instance, he is within a few feet of you, so he does not feel isolated. As long as you stop your work frequently in order to satisfy his needs, I feel the playpen is a reasonable place for him to spend short periods.

The only other occasion is if you live up one or two flights of stairs and do not feel able to carry him with you when you need to answer the front door. You obviously must not leave him on his own, even for a few seconds, and so here the playpen can be useful. But having said this, it would really be preferable that you carry him downstairs with you. The important point is not to feel that the front door bell, or the telephone for that matter, is an emergency and that you dash to answer it without first working out the safety of your baby. Babies always come before bells.

Make sure that any playpen you use conforms to safety requirements. It is useful to have one on wheels, so that you can take it from room to room.

Q **We have identical twin girls of eighteen months. I would like to encourage them to develop as individuals. Will it matter if I dress them differently? Or is it better to treat them indentically?**

You seem to want to decide a great deal for your twin girls rather than letting them choose how they dress and whether they would like to go to the same school. Being a twin is tremendous fun, and although some days they will want to dress differently, I think you will find that they often enjoy wearing the same clothes.

Twins have so many ways in which they can show their differences from other people. They are even likely to have their own special language and so be able to keep their parents out of their conversation. What fun that must be! Parents of twins should know that this is almost universal with twins, and that they are likely to talk normally later than average. Why bother to talk to adults when you've got your twin all to yourself!

You will not be able to encourage your twins to be more individualistic by anything you do. They are bound to see through your actions and then react against what it is that you are doing. Why are you so concerned about encouraging them to be individuals, anyway? They will be whatever nature planned for them, as long as you don't try to change them.

The closeness between twins is something unique and very precious to them. They will protect each other against the rest of the world, whatever the odds against them. My wife was one of twins, and she and her brother were so close that they never quarreled. She never appreciated this point

Left Identical twins usually enjoy dressing alike, and will probably be particularly close to each other. They may even develop their own peculiar language that the rest of the family cannot understand. Their rate of development, however, may not always be identical. Bottom left There are many programs that the under-fives will enjoy: but television should never be used simply as a means of keeping them occupied. Far better that you watch together so that any explanations necessary can be given and the subject of the program subsequently discussed.

Whether you read from a book or make one up, no matter: a bedtime story can provide a delightful conclusion to the child's day, and is an excellent way of changing the tempo.

until our children were born and they quarreled just like other children. Initially, this caused my wife great distress, because she did not realize that quarreling was usual among children.

From what I have said, I hope you will let the children decide about whether they dress alike or whether they go to the same school. I think most twins want to be together at school, and the reasons for separating them would be rare indeed. Starting school can be a very lonely experience, but not for twins. What is more, twins rarely get bullied because there is always the other one to come to the rescue.

Q Do you think that bedtime stories are important to children?

Bedtime should be fun and something to look forward to, and a story is a wonderful way for a parent and child to end the day together.

Bedtime stories provide an intimate occasion, and for some children may be the only time they really have a parent to themselves. They are also an important way of changing the tempo from the excitement of day play to the soporific land of

make-believe. I often wonder how children can be expected to switch off in the middle of an exciting game and go to bed and sleep almost in one go. In fact, I suspect that many sleep problems may actually relate to the absence of bedtime stories. How often does one hear a child being told, "Go to bed and go to sleep!" What a dull way to end the day.

You will soon learn what sort of story your child likes best, especially when he or she keeps asking for the same one again. Whether to read a story or make one up depends on you and your imagination but I would certainly include some of the classic children's books with pictures.

How long you spend on the story will also depend on you, except that sometimes you will find your child has fallen asleep before the end!

Q **Do you think it is possible for a four-year-old to watch too much television? Can this be harmful in any way?**

I am inclined to say no, because a four-year-old reacts to boredom so much more quickly than an adult does. If bored, he would fall asleep or go off and play. Adults, on the other hand, seem to get mesmerized by television so that they just can't switch it off. I think also that an adult watching a boring program always thinks it's bound to get interesting soon, which is partly why he continues to have it on.

Opinions have changed about eye strain, so that we no longer believe that too much television, or as it used to be said, too much reading, can strain the eyes.

I am, however, always concerned if the television comes to be used as a babysitter so that a mother can get on with her work. This certainly often happens with older children who get hooked on TV just like adults, but I don't believe that a child as young as four years of age would react in this way.

But having given these views, I very much hope that parents will spend time playing with their young children, rather than trying to keep them occupied with the television. That is not to say that a child of four won't learn from television, because many superb programs have been made for this age group. Best of all is for the child to watch with mother so that she can explain and talk about what has taken place and be immediately available to answer his questions.

Moreover, they can continue to discuss the program they have watched together after it has finished.

Q **Is it better for our baby to suck a pacifier rather than his fingers? Could it be harmful in any way?**

I believe it is much better for a baby to suck his thumb rather than a pacifier. My reason for this has nothing to do with hygiene, although in my medical training I was taught that pacifiers are dirty and should be discouraged for this reason.

My reason for not wanting pacifiers is that they block the mouth like a plug. The mouth of a baby is in many ways his most important opening. Out of it comes his early sounds and into it, at an early stage, go his fingers and toys as he begins to explore. This important stage of development is denied to a baby whose mouth is blocked with a pacifier.

It is natural for babies to want to suck, and it would seem that breastfed babies, who suck more than those on the bottle, get extra satisfaction this way so that they suck the thumb less. Pacifiers are dirty but so are thumbs, so I would not use that argument. However, a baby raised on a pacifier cries when it falls out of his mouth, whereas the thumb remains attached.

Pacifiers have one extra hazard since some mothers stick the end in honey before putting it in the baby's mouth. This increases the likelihood of dental decay. Worse still are the feeders that are attached to little reservoirs for syrupy solutions. They almost guarantee severe dental decay. Another occasional habit of mothers who use pacifiers is to lick them before placing in the baby's mouth. I tremble to think of all the bacteria that must be transferred in this way.

Q **I suspect that our five-year-old sometimes takes small change from my purse. I have occasionally noticed that coins are missing. What should I do about this?**

I have to ask first of all what has made you have these suspicions. Most people don't check their small change, so something must have led you to check in this way.

As for what you should do, my advice would be for you to ensure that you do not leave your purse lying around, so that your five-year-old has fewer opportunities. If, after this, it is clear that he has found your purse, say, in a drawer, and you are quite certain he has taken something, then it would be quite

reasonable to mention in a very gentle fashion that you have noticed that money is missing from your purse. In saying this, you have to be certain of your facts, but I do not suggest that you make a great thing about the whole episode. Try to make it easy for him to stop taking the money, perhaps by mentioning that you think someone is taking money from your purse behind your back, but not by accusing him directly.

Children feel very guilty about doing anything wrong, and it is important for you to work out why he should need to take this money, if this is the case. I once heard of a little girl who was denied candy by her parents, so she and her brother stole money from the mantelpiece in their parents' bedroom. Having bought and eaten the candy, they felt desperately guilty, so when they next had their allowance, they put back the money they had taken.

Q **Our four-year-old boy still insists on using a pacifier for quite long periods during the day. How can we break this habit before he starts school?**

Your use of the phrase "break the habit" tells me quite a bit about the strength of your feelings on the subject. And I am sure your son is aware of these feelings, which are bound to be causing him to react adversely.

It would be interesting to know how he came to rely on his pacifier in the first place. I imagine you would answer that you gave it to him for comfort when nothing else would calm him. But in fact children get much more comfort from being cuddled and are often calling out for this when a pacifier is thrust into the mouth and the habit is started.

It's also a pity that parents forget that children are actually born with a pacifier attached. It is not only far more effective for a child to suck his *thumb* for comfort than have to search for his pacifier. The thumb also never gets lost!

In my early training as a doctor, I was taught not to favor pacifiers because they were dirty and a cause of infection. But that is not the reason I am against them now. To my mind, they act like a plug—blocking what, for the first year or two of life, is one of the most important openings in the body. A young child naturally uses his mouth for exploration. You will remember, I am sure, how your own child used to put his toys, or anything else for that matter, into his mouth.

The young child also needs to experiment with early sounds, and to learn that, by changing the shape of his mouth and moving his tongue, he can alter these in his early attempts at learning to talk. It is sad to think that the mouth may be plugged by a pacifier so that sounds cannot come out and objects cannot be explored.

A child who is spastic and has never gotten his thumb into his mouth is helped to do so by his physiotherapist. You should see the excitement on his face when he first achieves this new experience and how he then enjoys practicing on his own.

Understanding all these aspects will help you appreciate the problem lying ahead before you "break the habit." Why are you so eager to achieve this before he goes to school? I expect you would answer that he may get teased but that would probably make him change the habit more quickly than anything else.

The main thing is to play it cool so that he doesn't fight against your determination to rid him of this habit that you started. And, with the next child, try not to give him a pacifier in the first place. Be subtle so that, instead of actually telling him to take his pacifier out of his mouth, you play a game that necessitates the use of speech and pretend you can't understand him if he talks with his pacifier in place. Alternatively, you could try losing it.

Q **Why is peek-a-boo such a universally popular game with babies? Why do they find it such fun?**

I imagine there are many reasons why a baby enjoys a game of peek-a-boo. Perhaps most of all he delights in the undivided attention of an adult, just as he does in the game of getting an adult repeatedly to pick up the toy he keeps dropping.

When the world is so full of things you do not understand, it must be very exciting that someone who has just left you feeling bewildered by the way they have suddenly disappeared—and bewilderment is the main feature of the child's face at this point—should suddenly reappear as if by magic. I suspect it is this element of magic that is most exciting and gives the greatest pleasure.

Usually, in peek-a-boo, the adult's face is beaming with a smile, and young children reciprocate smiles in such a marvelous way that the adult is urged on to still more smiles. Tests with cardboard cutouts show very different responses to smiling adult faces and solemn ones, which sometimes may almost make the child cry.

Babies love to learn, and the game of peek-a-boo provides many such learning opportunities, as well as being fun. Moreover, provided the end is always happy, I think that possibly a baby actually may enjoy being slightly frightened by the prospect of his mother disappearing. It's rather like an older child seeing how close he dares to get to the edge of a cliff.

Q **Amanda is always biting her nails. They look dreadful. How can we stop her from continuing with this habit?**

Nail-biting is a habit much like thumb-sucking, which commonly reflects anxiety. It is also brought on by boredom. So there are two areas for you to explore as possible causes. Finding and dealing with the cause is the way to stop the habit.

Very often someone else in the family—mother or father, for example—bites their nails, too. If this is the case, you will get nowhere until they stop.

On no account paint the nails with bitter aloes or some other unpleasant substance. This will encourage your child to defy you, since all she has to do is to wipe it off.

And try not to say "Don't do that" when you see her biting her nails. She is probably trying very hard to stop, and being scolded doesn't help. Far better, try to distract her so that she takes up some other activity.

Most children do want their hands to look good. This is an aspect that can be exploited in a girl by letting her have her own bottle of nail polish. She will want to show this off to her friends but not on bitten nails, so she will do everything to let them grow. One important warning: the teacher must help rather than scold the child for using nail polish. Explain in advance that it is "medical nail polish" and you will be sure to get the school's cooperation.

Q **My child who is seven months old has started to cling to me and is frightened of everyone else, including his father. Is this something we should be concerned about? What could we be doing to give him more confidence?**

This is a normal reaction of children between about the age of seven to ten months. It is sometimes called the "stranger reaction." The child has reached the age when he can differentiate his mother from everyone else. He feels totally safe with her, but goes through a phase of feeling unsafe with everyone else.

It is most important that all parents should be aware of this, because fathers in particular may feel very hurt if their child reacts against them.

Most children go through the stage of experiencing a "stranger reaction", only feeling safe with their mothers. But this is generally a fairly short-lived phase. Far right Not stepping on the pavement cracks is a very common childhood habit, often reinforced by parental behavior.

Father or mother scolds the child for the habit, and the child reacts by disobeying. Change your tactics and play the game, too. A little understanding is required. The child may be convinced that something dreadful will happen if he happens to step on a crack.

It is essential to understand what is happening and to give the child the safety he is asking for. In other words, it would be wrong to make him go to his father or anyone else until he feels safe enough to do so. This phase usually only lasts a few weeks. As long as you do not try to push him through it faster than his own pace, you and he will emerge at the other end without any permanent problems.

Q Our five-year-old boy seems to be obsessed about not stepping on pavement cracks. How can we stop him being so concerned about this? Is it some sort of obsession?

This question takes me back to A.A. Milne's book *Winnie the Pooh* because Christopher Robin vividly describes the need not to walk on the cracks.

I would think there are few children who have not gone through this phase. I certainly did, and even now I sometimes find myself avoiding the cracks. I suspect there are many adults who do the same.

So I hope I can convince you that your child's habit is normal even though it may seem to have reached obsessional proportions. I wonder if you have even told him not to do it. If you have, you will have been encouraging him to continue without meaning to do so, since any normal child would disobey his mother if she said something silly like that. Moreover, being told not to do it increases his difficulty in breaking the habit by making him think about it more.

You must start by asking yourself what is wrong with what he is doing. I would be very surprised if you can find a good reason. The problem really is that it annoys you. He knows that and so goes on doing it.

Try changing your tactics entirely and play the game with him. You'll then have fun together, and when you get tired he will probably agree to play another game, or to stop and give you a rest. But

if he continues, on no account tell him to stop. See it through his eyes. He will almost certainly have told himself that something terrible will happen to him if he makes a mistake and steps on a crack.

Q **I have heard about something called "three months colic." What exactly is this?**

The term "three months colic" is used to describe the condition of those babies in the first three months of life who cry more than the average, do not settle down, and are thoroughly miserable. Those who use the term state that they know the baby has "colic" (spasm of the intestines) because he keeps drawing his legs up when he cries. But all babies do that unless prevented by a blanket.

Those who use the term also often incriminate gas as part of the problem, stating that there is excessive gas in the baby's intestines. The fact that the baby often passes flatus from the rectum while drawing up his legs is used to support this idea, but the reason he passes gas is the increase in intra-abdominal pressure that accompanies crying.

All in all, you will gather that I do not find three months colic a satisfactory term. I believe it was invented by someone who could not find out why a healthy baby was crying, so he told the mother it was colic. She was then satisfied once she had a name for the problem, even though it didn't mean anything special or make him better any more quickly.

I believe "colic" is one of those terms that, like "teething," bear no relation to the truth but are given to mothers to explain something the doctor or nurse doesn't understand. The concept of excess gas causing crying is to my mind totally fallacious. I base this dogmatic statement on the fact that large areas of the world have never even heard of colic and do not go through the traditional maneuvres of English and American mothers in order to burp the baby.

I first became interested in the geographical aspect of gas when my sister-in-law, from Czechoslovakia, had her first baby in London, where she was taught how to burp the baby. She had her second baby in Prague and at that time there was no gas in Czechoslovakia. So the doctors and nurses could not understand why she banged her baby's back after meals!

I have traveled widely in developing countries and rarely find anyone who has heard of burping unless they have had a western upbringing.

If you X-ray the abdomen of the baby, you will find that the intestines are half full of gas and half full of fluid, but you also find exactly the same in adults!

The word "colic" is used as an alternative to screaming for which gas is given as the cause. I have no belief in this explanation, and I dissuade mothers from wasting time and from upsetting their babies by holding them upright and banging their backs after meals. I have found no problem with babies who are not treated this way. They are much more comfortable than their counterparts who are burped.

I can think of nothing more uncomfortable after enjoying a delicious breastfeed than to be thumped when really you want to be cuddled. Moreover, some of these poor babies have their feeding stopped in the middle so that their mothers can burp them. Until this magic sound is achieved, no further food is given. I have sometimes thought that, if only it were silent, the magic noise of the burp would no longer be needed to calm the mothers.

What, then, is the explanation of the baby's discomfort and crying at the end of the feeding? I think that some are taken off the breast a while before they have finished their feeding. It is normal for a baby to take a rest and maybe sometimes to go to sleep during a feeding. If this is misunderstood and the baby is stopped from feeding, he will naturally cry. Some of these poor babies are then described as "having gas."

We have a lot to learn from developing countries where babies are fed for the long periods they need. Carried on the back as they so often are in these parts of the world, they can be swung round to the breast whenever they want to feed. Crying is exceptional, as it is in the baby of any calm western mother who feeds her baby for as long and as often as he asks.

The trick is not to rush the baby through his feeding and to give him a long cuddle before putting him down. Then he has time to burp if he wishes. "Colic" is more common in bottle-fed babies, and I suspect this is due to short hurried feedings, a period of burping and then the expectation that he will go straight to sleep in his crib.

Babies are a very accurate indication of their mothers' feelings, and there is no doubt that a tense mother can convey anxiety to her baby. I remember an occasion when a mother was quietly holding her baby in my consulting room, waiting for me to finish writing up the notes of the previous baby. I turned to her when I had finished and asked how her baby was. As she spoke, I watched her grow tense and her hands clenched. Her words of reply were, "He's very tense." At the same moment, he gave out a shriek, almost as though an electric current had gone through him.

My aim is to get away from mechanical explanations for the crying of babies. They are not meant to cry, and if they are healthy and not hungry, the most likely cause lies in their sensitivity to their mothers' feelings. I always try to explain this with the utmost tact, just in case a mother believes I am saying it is her fault.

Fault in terms of childrearing is not a term I even consider. I want mothers to understand their babies, and to appreciate why they behave as they do. I would never blame them, but it is very difficult to prevent them from feeling blamed.

If I can successfully get over to parents what I have mentioned here, I find I can almost always help them and get rid of the baby's symptoms. I never use medicines for so-called colic, and I never use that meaningless phrase "he will grow out of it."

Q Do you think we should always reward good behavior?

I am sure you like praise, just like everyone else. The same goes for your children. It also helps them know they have done the right thing when they get praised. How awful life would be if we only got punished for our misdeeds and never had any praise! And yet this is the way quite a lot of parents continue to handle their children.

The importance of praise for good behavior is shown by the fact that it has now become a part of the standard treatment for behavior problems used by many child psychologists for behavior problems and is known as "behavior modification." Children want to please their parents, and praise is one of the principal ways in which you can show your pleasure in them. Consequently, they are much more likely to do those things that lead to praise rather than to punishment.

Sadly, busy mothers often do exactly the reverse. The following situation is not uncommon. While a child is playing quietly, his mother feels she can get on with her work. After a time, the child gets bored and calls out to his mother, though she probably takes no notice until he shouts. This means that she is in fact teaching him to shout by more or less saying "I'm not going to take any notice of you if you don't shout." She does not realize what she herself has brought about, and then complains to her doctor that her child is always shouting or that he refuses to obey her unless she shouts. She is quite unaware that it is *she* who has conditioned him to shout when he wants something.

From all this, you can see the ideal way to get the best from your children. Praise their good behavior and disregard the bad. Although you are very busy in the kitchen, pop out as often as you can to look at his painting and tell him how clever he is. You will reap the rewards, too.

Q Our three-year-old is very clumsy. How can we set about improving his coordination?

There is more than one reason for being clumsy, so you must try to identify into which group your child falls. Many normal children get labeled as "clumsy" when it is merely that they do everything at full speed and haven't allowed themselves time not to catch the edge of the door as they dash through. Sometimes parents are just expecting too much.

I do not deny that some young children are more clumsy than the average, but unless this is severe, I would believe it is part of the range of normal behavior. As your child grows up, his actions are likely to become more accurate, but I am sure you know some normal, intelligent adults who are just that bit clumsier than the average.

There is, however, a group of children who are pathologically clumsy. I think of them as the mild end of cerebral palsy (spastic). Most have normal intelligence but have great difficulty with fine finger movements so that fiddly tasks, like doing up buttons, are especially difficult.

Such children can be greatly helped by an occupational therapist who has been trained to work with children. She can teach the child tricks so that he carefully follows the movements of his legs and hands. He will, for instance, acquire better foot control by practicing walking on lines, squares, or footprints. Getting him to draw a line so that it never touches two parallel lines that simulate the edges of a road may also help develop his skills.

Many clumsy children can be greatly helped by experts. It is vital that such children are identified and receive treatment because clumsiness causes much unhappiness and a lot of teasing. Teachers must be on the look out for children with poor coordination and ensure they receive help, much of which can be given in school by ordinary teachers, additionally trained in the special needs of these children.

Q **Tina, who will soon be five, seems to have an imaginary friend. She talks to her almost constantly, and tells us stories about her. Is this something to be concerned about?**

It could be that you have a child of above average intelligence and with the gift of imagination. She has the ability to conjure up an imaginary friend, and perhaps they do exciting things together and enjoy themselves. Your daughter is also probably seldom, if ever, lonely because she always has her imaginary friend to keep her company. It is interesting that I have never heard of a small child having an imaginary enemy.

Do bear in mind that the worst thing you could do is to suggest that she is being stupid and that her friend is not real. To her, the friend is *very* real, even though deep down she knows that her friend cannot be seen by other people. In a way, that makes for extra fun; to have someone all to yourself in whom you can confide and sometimes to be able to tell the friend how unfair or difficult Mommy or Daddy has been must be wonderful. What a great safety valve it would be if we all had such a friend!

It is actually quite a common occurrence, and some children use their pets as confidantes. In growing up, however, your daughter will gradually grow away from the need for this imaginary friend. Meanwhile, I hope you can see that far from being a cause for concern, this fantasy is something you, too, might even enjoy for a while.

Q **How can we best stop our five-year-old picking his nose so much?**

There can be few children who have not picked their noses, but the major problem is that adults are so liable to draw attention to the habit that the effect is to perpetuate rather than stop it.

Children perform to audiences and enjoy testing their relatives. My advice is to walk away from the child if attempts to distract him fail.

But do remember that a child who picks his nose may have inserted a foreign body, such as a bead. This is particularly likely if discharge comes from one nostril only. If nothing is visible to your naked eye, ask your doctor to check with a special light. If he still has doubts, he may decide to X-ray the nose.

I find myself interested that you should use the phrase "so much," as though you will allow him to do it a little. Your object must be to stop the habit altogether, but nonaggressive methods will be far more successful than battles.

Q **Our two-year-old seems to be very contrary most of the time. What do you suggest we do ?**

My question to you is "What do you mean by contrary?" I assume you mean that your child is difficult and doesn't do what you want. There is an expression that I do not like—"the terrible two's." Possibly, this has been used to you about your child.

During the first year of life, you cannot expect a child to understand what you want in an adult sense, but by the time a child is two, some parents expect a great deal of their child, and particularly that he should understand what they mean when they say "no." From the two-year-old's point of view, this is a particularly exciting time of life because not only is he learning a great deal about the world, but he has discovered that his parents seem to get very worked up about some actions of his. He has entered what we often call the "negativistic" phase. This means that he will react against your wishes in those areas where you show particular concern. If you are anxious that he eats all his food, then he will probably start to play with it and certainly will not eat it all. On the other hand, if you are concerned about toilet-training, then he is likely to hold onto his stools—in other words, to be a "stool-holder" and not have his bowels open into the toilet when you want him to do so. Some children become "word-holders" and develop a grunt language of their own when their parents are particularly eager to make them talk properly.

The areas in which parents are likely to pressurize their child are those in which they themselves were pressurized. All this means that you have to work hard to understand your child's needs. You will find the more you understand him, the less you will need to exert strong discipline.

Good Health

Q How can I be sure that my child will not be left with pock marks after chickenpox?

Chickenpox is one of the most infectious of childhood illnesses, but fortunately it is seldom serious. However, the blisters that are typical of the illness are extremely irritating, especially in the very young. This leads the child to scratch, which can cause secondary infection of the spots so that permanent scarring results.

Fortunately, there is a very simple method of removing this inflammation. You can buy potassium permanganate crystals from the pharmacist. Put a small handful of these in a bath of water, so that the water becomes a reasonably mauve color. Your child is then allowed to soak in the bath for a few minutes. He probably won't want to come out because the liquid will remove the irritation. Don't be surprised if it leaves the skin brown, especially at the sites of the blisters. Once the blisters have become a deep brown, they lose their capacity to irritate.

One practical point: potassium permanganate stains the bath tub. You can get the color out by using sodium hypochlorite.

You may hear it advised that your child should wear gloves in order to prevent him scratching. My feeling is that they are so uncomfortable and hot that they may hinder rather than help. But certainly his nails should be kept as short as possible to reduce the ability to scratch. In any case, I hope that scratching will not be a problem because of potassium permanganate baths. Potassium permanganate is also called Condy's fluid.

Q Is it true that certain diseases can be caused by pets? What can we do to prevent them?

It is certainly true that pets can cause some diseases, but on the whole I think the problem has been exaggerated. I hope you will not be put off getting a pet for your child because of the risk of disease.

It may be helpful to look at the many anxieties that commonly arise as far as pets are concerned. Parents are so often worried that their children may catch worms from pets, but I hope that they will have their dogs dewormed for the pets' own health anyway, so that this will not be a problem.

The most serious worm is called "toxocara." Dogs and cats may be infected, and may pass stools that contain the eggs. Although a child could be infected by his own pet, contamination of his hands while playing in a park is the more likely source of transfer. The eggs are transferred when he puts his hands into his mouth, and they hatch into larvae in the child's intestine. From there, they can pass into any of the body's organs, and cause disease.

Dog and cat fleas may also cause skin rashes, due to an allergic reation rather than a bite. It is also possible to catch ringworm from a dog or cat, although some types of ringworm affect only human beings.

Asthma, meanwhile, is often due to sensitivity to a mite that lives in house dust. It can, of course, get into the fur of a pet, but is easily eliminated with use of a special powder that your pharmacist or vet will supply.

If a child is bitten by a dog, he should be seen by a doctor. The disease which is most greatly feared in the United States is rabies, which has been kept out of Great Britain by quarantine laws. Treatment is to inject antiserum around the cleaned wound and to give a course of rabies vaccination.

The other disease that causes great anxiety in this respect is tetanus: and although this is now exceptionally rare, it has to be considered following a bite. As long as your child has had a tetanus immunization, there is no problem since he will be given an extra shot and this will provide a complete safeguard. It is, of course, important that you should have his immunization book with its records easily available so that you can take it with you to the doctor or the hospital. If a child has not been immunized against tetanus, a decision must be made by the doctor as to whether he has ATS (anti-tetanic serum). This was once used a great deal, but now that the risk of tetanus is less and we know that there can sometimes be a reaction to ATS, it is less often prescribed. The doctor will certainly put your child on penicillin, which kills the tetanus, so there should be no problem.

Very occasionally, a cat can be infected with a virus that produces cat-scratch fever, although the pet seems quite well. A few days after the scratch, the child becomes ill, the scratch itself is inflamed and, very typically, the lymph gland in the area matching the site of the scratch is large and tender. Consequently, a scratch on the arm would produce a large lymph gland in the armpit, whereas a scratch on the leg would produce a swollen gland in the groin. Fortunately, this is very rare, but I would suggest that if your cat does scratch your child, you should check that the scratch does not become inflamed and that the child remains well.

Psittacosis is a virus disease of birds, and children may catch the disease from their parakeets or canaries. However, the danger is now slight because birds at risk arriving from abroad are placed in quarantine before being offered for sale as family pets.

A pet can be a great source of joy to a child and as long as basic rules of hygiene are observed, you should in no way let fear of disease put you off bringing a pet into the family circle.

Q Is there any harm in letting our four-year-old drink tea and coffee? He seems to enjoy them.

I presume you are worried that the caffeine in tea or coffee might harm your child by unnatural stimulation. I have never known a toddler or any child show adverse effects from tea or coffee and I would certainly let him have these beverages if he enjoys them, although it is less common for a child to do so.

It is all right to let your child make his own choice, whether milk, juices or just plain water. The only point made nowadays is that a pint of milk a day is too much because of its high fat content.

Q Why does our three-year-old get hiccups so often?

Some children certainly do get hiccups more often than others. One prevalent lay theory is that it is because they bolt their food, but of course lots of children do this and don't get hiccups. They are not dangerous, although they can be very exhausting, especially for adults.

The reason for hiccups is spasm of the diaphragm. This is quite common even before birth, and mothers usually have no difficulty in differentiating fetal movement and fetal hiccups because hiccups are so regular and induce a similar feeling each time they occur, whereas fetal movements are varied in timing and strength. I am particularly interested by babies who, having had intrauterine hiccups that always occurred at the same time, usually early evening, continued to have them at a similar time for the first few weeks after birth.

Whereas adults usually find hiccups very uncomfortable, babies are not put out by them and continue to nurse placidly. Giving a feeding often stops the hiccups.

As for stopping an attack of hiccups in older children or adults, one method—which my mother taught me and which has never failed—is to give the sufferer a glass of water. He or she should keep sipping while you stand behind and press the little piece of cartilage in front of the earhole so that it closes the hole. It is important to keep the mouth closed meanwhile. This method of stopping an attack of hiccups probably works by altering the pressure in the esophagus.

My first success with this method was as a medical student. After a major operation for a gastric ulcer, a middle-aged man had an extremely painful and exhausting attack of hiccups that had already lasted twenty-four hours. The doctor had prescribed all sorts of medicines but without success. He agreed to my trying my method which worked the first time. The longest attack of hiccups I have ever met was in a girl of eight who had them for six days. They stopped immediately when I applied the treatment but they started up again after half an hour. However, the second time the effect was permanent.

Q I have noticed that our four-year-old son sometimes uses very unrealistic colors for his drawings. This is worrying us.

I would think it most unlikely that your child is color-blind. It is natural for him to practice with all sorts of color combinations and he is indicating an imaginative approach. In fact, he is actually showing that he is *not* color-blind since he would not get pleasure from combinations that he could not differentiate.

A child who is color-blind muddles or misnames colors, but this does not seem to be the problem with your child. I don't suggest you try to test him yet because he is too young, and you will only increase your anxiety if he makes mistakes on the test.

Color-blindness is, incidentally, much more common in boys than in girls. A major degree of color-blindness would be obvious by the age of five when you would notice that he persistently misnames certain colors, especially red and green. Tests are usually carried out at the first school medical examination at the age of five years. A special book is used with a mass of different colored dots on each page. The normal child can pick out a figure composed of dots of one color "hidden" among the maze of dots, whereas this is invisible to someone who is color-blind.

Q Our baby has prickly heat. How should we best treat the condition?

Prickly heat is a skin condition that results from excessive sweating and is therefore common in the tropics, especially in those who are fair-skinned. It occurs both in children and in adults, although the tendency to sweat varies greatly from one person to another.

The rash comprises red spots and blisters that

itch terribly. They occur especially in folds of skin and therefore are commonest in the neck, armpits, and groin, as well as on the face and trunk.

Both the prevention and the cure lie in frequent baths, followed by a change of clothes. These should be loose and made of cotton to absorb the sweat. Sometimes it helps to leave off the clothes as long as there is no risk of sunburn. Talcum powder helps to keep down the sweat and calamine lotion is also very soothing.

Do everything you can to keep your child from sweating without limiting his activities. Babies when outdoors should be left where there is a gentle breeze or in the shade of a tree; when indoors, an electric fan or airconditioning should be used whenever possible.

Q What would you recommend as the best way to give our toddler medicine?

You are obviously expecting trouble, which is understandable, but the manufacturers now go to immense lengths to make medicines not only palatable but also attractive in color for children. You may even find that your child positively relishes his medicine.

But despite all this, your toddler may have a natural suspicion about something new, especially if he is not feeling well. Your approach is very important since if you look as though you are anticipating a problem, you will almost certainly get it. On no account start cajoling or bribing; he will take advantage of you mercilessly.

Probably the best thing you can do is to make it clear that you are not going to stand nonsense but are not of course going to force it down his throat or hold his nose.

You are more likely to be prescribed a medicine rather than tablets for your toddler. If you are given tablets, it is best to crush them and give them in a spoonful of fruit juice, or hidden in jam or marmalade on a spoon.

I am not in favor of a reward of a sweet after taking medicine. For his teeth's sake, I hope there are no sweets in your house, so that you would not resort to this technique. At any rate, do all you can to make no mention of rewards.

Q Is it safe to give our four-year-old a pain-killer such as aspirin if he has stomach ache?

No. The reason is that you might make the pain go away but the underlying diagnosis has not been discovered. The pain could be due to acute appendicitis which thereby becomes masked.

Doctors have a rule that they give no pain relievers for acute abdominal pain until a diagnosis has been made and a plan of treatment formulated. Masking disease by giving pain-relieving medicine is hazardous.

You do not mention whether you are referring to a single attack of abdominal pain in an ill child or the more common recurrent abdominal pain in a child who is not ill. This pain is similar to the butterflies in the stomach felt by adults at times of anxiety.

The abdomen, especially in children, is a very sensitive area as far as reflecting feelings is concerned. Whereas adults are more likely to get headaches when they are stressed and exhausted, children more often experience a pain in the abdomen. This is actually due to feeling the waves of peristalsis that drive the food along the intestines from mouth to rectum. Normally we are not conscious of this constant physiological machine working away, but anxiety can create stronger waves that reach the level of consciousness. I explain to children that they are feeling the food going round the corners in the intestine and use drawings to help in the explanation.

Once a child can understand the reason for his pain, particularly if his mother loses her anxiety as well, the pain recurs less frequently and usually disappears quite soon. On the other hand, if a mother gives the child an aspirin every time, it may make the pain go but he will probably come to rely on aspirin and think of the pain as due to an illness that requires medicine for a cure.

Some parents are always dishing out medicines to their children and themselves. Such children come to rely on medicine and pills and are far more likely to continue with their bouts of pain compared with the child who can understand the workings of his stomach and intestines.

Q I have heard that it can be dangerous for a small baby to get diarrhea. Is that so?

It is very true that diarrhea can be dangerous. This is because the child becomes dehydrated from loss of fluid, causing an upset in the body's chemistry, which is more delicately balanced in a baby. Risk to a baby's life is also far greater as a result of diarrhea than it is in an adult.

For some reason, which I believe to be historical, parents are often more concerned with a supposed need for a daily bowel action than by diarrhea. I must emphasize that diarrhea—especially watery diarrhea in a baby—is very dangerous.

You should judge the risk to the baby by the effect it has on him. A baby who passes a few loose motions, but who remains happy and still

A child's stomach pains are sometimes associated with fear or anxiety: so that whereas you may suspect that your child is pretending to be ill because he or she does not want to go to school, the pain could be very real.

eats and drinks, is in no danger. The serious form of diarrhea is associated with loss of appetite and, worse still, with vomiting as well. Such a baby soon becomes dehydrated causing the eyes to become sunken, activity to lessen, the skin to be inelastic, and the mouth to be dry. A whimpering cry is common.

Such a baby must be seen immediately by the doctor. On no account wait until the next morning. If he is not vomiting, he will probably take fluid by mouth. But if this is refused and especially if he is vomiting, he will need to go to the hospital for intravenous feeding.

A recent advance has been the emphasis on rehydration by mouth using a special mixture of glucose and salt supplied in a sachet for dissolving in water, as stated on the packet. Because of the chemical content, the water is better absorbed and less likely to be vomited so that there is now a worldwide campaign to encourage the use of "oral rehydration." The preparation is available from pharmacies without the need for a prescription. In the tropics, where the danger is greatest, they are freely supplied in village dispensaries.

Q **What is the best way to take our baby's temperature? Is it safe to use an ordinary thermometer?**

I suggest that you use the rectal route, which is simple and safe. A special thermometer is required that has a stubby end for the mercury so that there is no risk of breakage. Shake the thermometer to ensure that the mercury is at the

bottom and grease the tip so that it slides in easily.

Place the baby on the bed on his back and hold both ankles with your left hand. Bend his knees up to his tummy with your right hand so that the anus is exposed. The end of the thermometer should be inserted for about one inch. Leave it in position for at least two minutes. (One minute is sometimes suggested but this is not always adequate). To read the thermometer, roll it round to get the mercury to show to best advantage. Wash the thermometer after use in cold water. It could burst if you used hot water.

Babies can develop very low temperatures which is why hospitals always use a low-reading thermometer. This has its low point marked at 85° F instead of 95° F as in the ordinary thermometers used for adults and ensures that, for a baby whose temperature is below 95° F, a fallacious result is not given if the mercury fails to drop to the true low-point. You would be wise to use a similar low-reading thermometer for your baby.

It is natural to be a bit scared the first time, so get a nurse in the hospital to let you take your baby's temperature on one or two occasions. The use of an ordinary thermometer in the armpit or groin is an alternative method but it is much less accurate.

It is normal for a child's temperature to vary considerably in the course of the day, so the concept of "normal" being a straight line as on temperature charts is totally erroneous. I am constantly striving to help parents get away from the notion of judging whether their child is ill by the length of a column of mercury that might be inaccurate in any case. Decide on the basis of knowing your child and act accordingly.

Children's medicine is today usually very palatable and attractive in color, so that you should not encounter too much of a problem in getting your toddler to take whatever has been prescribed. Try to avoid rewarding your child for taking the medicine and do not offer candy, for the sake of his or her teeth.

If in doubt, contact your doctor. In any case you will soon become skilled at detecting a rise in temperature by feeling your child's forehead.

For years I have asked doctors when phoned by a mother about her child not to ask for the temperature. The mother knows whether she needs the doctor's help, yet by his question he is helping breed a race of mothers who feel scared to telephone the doctor because the child does not have a rise in temperature. A child can be very ill with a "normal" temperature.

Q **What sort of foods do you think constitute a good varied and balanced diet for a five-year-old?**

I find myself much less complicated about diet than so many other people who write books about children. I can't believe you spend a great deal of time working out whether you and your husband are having a good varied diet. I suspect you eat what you fancy—except I hope you watch that your diet doesn't contain too many fattening and sweet foods.

I would adopt the same approach for your child, who I hope is on the same diet as you are. She is then much more likely to eat without problems. It is the mother who emphasizes the need for a clean plate who produces the child who refuses to eat up everything on her plate.

In the same way, I don't find myself emphasizing the phrase "balanced diet." Your child of five who is eating the same foods that you are with meat, fish, eggs, and cheese for protein, fruit and vegetables, and not too much carbohydrate by way of bread, potatoes, and cakes is, I am sure, getting just what she needs. And you don't need to give her extra vitamins.

You can judge that a child is not lacking in her diet by the fact that she is energetic. The starved children of the Third World are inactive so that the body doesn't waste any calories in energy.

My advice is for you to take meals in your stride without emphasizing the importance of any particular food. You'll then find your child will eat like a horse, rather than becoming a fussy eater.

Q **Our baby has been diagnosed as having celiac disease. Can you explain exactly what this means? Is it a lifelong condition? What sort of diet will she have to follow? Will the condition cause great problems?**

Celiac disease results from an abnormality of the lining of the intestine that prevents the absorption of *gluten*, a constituent of protein. The disease is present from birth but doesn't show until the child eats food containing gluten. The first food containing gluten is usually cereal, which is often first given at about three to six months of age.

This causes the baby to become ill and he starts to pass watery stools that change to the very typical pale, offensive-smelling, and bulky stools containing a lot of fat. The child may also vomit and he will certainly lose weight, so that his limbs look like sticks, the abdomen protrudes, and the buttocks get very thin and hang in folds.

Treatment lies in giving a diet from which all gluten is excluded. The dietician at the hospital will help you produce all sorts of interesting dishes made with gluten-free flour. Special bread and crackers made in the right way can be bought or made by you.

Don't think of the diet as a family disaster. The easiest thing will be for the whole family to go on to a gluten-free diet. I once spent a few days with a pediatrician who had celiac disease and it was only as I was leaving after a luxurious weekend, with superb cooking, that he told me I had been on a gluten-free diet all the time!

Celiac disease is a lifelong condition, so it is essential that the person who has the disorder remain on the gluten-free diet for life. If not, he or she will get bouts of abdominal pain, sickness, and loose stools, as well as feeling unwell. This may occur at any time, but especially after an alcoholic binge or in association with pregnancy.

Celiac disease also increases the risk of intestinal cancer when much older—a risk that is prevented by a gluten-free diet—so make sure the diet is strictly kept, although during adolescence and the teens it is especially difficult to tolerate standing out as someone different.

Q **How can we tell whether our four-year-old son really has a stomach ache or whether he is pretending, as we think happened yesterday? Could he possibly be using it as an excuse?**

I think that children very rarely pretend that they have abdominal pain when they haven't. So I believe what you are really wondering is whether he has some organic disease like appendicitis or whether the pain is what doctors call "functional" meaning that there is no underlying disease. In that case, the child is not making up the pain but he is feeling the workings of his stomach.

I am sure you sometimes get a headache, yet I don't believe I would see anything wrong if I looked at your brain, even under the microscope. But that doesn't mean to say you are making it up. I am quite certain you are not.

Functional pains are usually associated with fear, anxiety, and worry. If your child gets a pain just before going to school, it is likely that there is a lesson that day that he hates. But he *has* also got a stomach ache.

Children feel anxiety pains in their stomach more than anywhere else, whereas grownups feel them in the head and get frontal headaches mostly. Let's work out what is happening inside the child. When he eats, food goes down his gullet (esophagus) and into his stomach. It then travels along twenty feet or more of intestine. While passing along the intestinal tube, most of the food is absorbed and will be used for him to grow and to provide energy. What is left over is passed when the bowels are opened. The intestines are coiled on themselves to get into the abdominal cavity. This means that their contents have to go around corners. Sometimes this makes them gurgle, much to the individual's embarrassment. The child may even *feel* the contents being pushed along by little intestinal waves known as *peristalsis*. It is this process that gives him the pain. Anxiety as a cause of stomach ache is in fact very common, and we even sometimes talk of the feeling as butterflies in the stomach.

If your child is otherwise well and especially if he is the anxious sort, you don't have to look further for the cause of the pain. But you must make sure you know he has it and is not making it up. I draw diagrams for the children to show how their stomachs work and why they get the pain. Once they understand all about it, they are no longer frightened by the pain. It feels less serious and comes less often.

The worst thing a doctor can do is to suggest there is no cause or say he can't find one. These statements are alarming and lead to misunderstandings by parents and child. Make quite sure your child understands the mechanism along the lines I have explained and you should find the pain stops being a problem. I always enjoy seeing children with the symptom because they respond so well to an explanation that they understand.

Q **Our child is hard of hearing. Do you think that we should send him to a special school?**

Before a decision is made as to whether your hard-of-hearing child should go to a special school, much more information is needed.

The phrase "hard of hearing" suggests partial rather than complete deafness, but in either case the presence of deafness must be proved by hearing tests. Next, the cause of his deafness must be discovered and, if possible, treated. Since he is of school age, I hope that his partial hearing loss was detected a long time ago. It is essential that deafness of any degree be discovered early in order to reduce the disability by appropriate treatment and in order to achieve optimal speech. (The phrase "deaf-mute" refers to a child whose deafness was not diagnosed so that he could not learn to speak.) Hearing is essential for the development of speech. This is why a deaf child given appropriate hearing aids cannot immediately speak. He has to learn to hear first.

If there is any doubt about the child's ability to hear, he will be referred to an audiologist (a medical specialist in diseases of the ear) for a more technical hearing test.

The commonest cause of partial deafness is middle ear infection due to "glue ear." The condition occurs most often in preschool children.

Decongestant nose drops may be tried but most cases require the removal of adenoids and the insertion of air tubes, called grommets, through the ear drum. Perfect hearing can usually be restored. These function like the eustachian tube that leads from the back of the throat to the middle ear. Restoration of air flow in the middle ear allows it to heal and no longer to produce "glue." These tubes should remain in for about six to twelve months.

However, it doesn't sound as though this is the cause in your child. It is more likely that his deafness is due to an abnormality of the hearing apparatus from birth. This commonly affects the nerves and is sometimes inherited. Hearing aids will be tried but are not always successful.

He will need speech training from a specialized teacher of the deaf, combined with help from a speech therapist. Opinions differ about the relative merits of lipreading and sign language, but probably a combination of both is best. In any case, a child is going to use signs whether taught these or not.

Finally, I have reached your question. Whether or not he should attend a special school depends on the severity of his hearing loss, the school facilities available locally, the advice of the teacher and the specialist helping him, and also what you, as his parents, feel is best for him and what *he* wants.

Ideally a child with a handicap should be given special help in an ordinary school. But such facilities for deaf children are limited, in which case he will need to go to a special school. The answer can be reached only by a team discussion with all concerned in order to help you make up your mind as to what sort of school would be preferable. The final decision is yours, but I hope you will take the advice of the specialists.

Q **What is the cause of cold sores? Why does our child seem to get them so often? Can they be prevented in any way? How should we treat them?**

Cold sores are due to infection with a virus called *herpes simplex*. The first attack causes painful ulcers throughout the mouth that last between seven and ten days. During this time, the child feels very miserable and unwell because of pain from the ulcers. Drinking is also painful, although the child may be thirsty.

Your doctor may prescribe some idoxuridine as a paint or drops to speed up the healing process. Your child will then be back to full health. Any weight lost during the acute illness will soon be regained. However, from now on he will be liable to cold sores whenever he has a cold or is feeling run down for any reason. This is because the virus does not disappear completely from the body but is living in the roots of the nerves that supply the edges of the mouth. Consequently, whenever the child's resistance is lowered by illness, he is likely to have an attack of cold sores, lasting about ten days. These start as blisters that soon become broken and sometimes get infected. They are not as painful as the original attack, but are certainly sore. It may be best to let them dry on their own, though

If you suspect that your child may have eaten plants or berries of any kind, it would be wise to take him either to the hospital emergency department or to your doctor right away. Certain seeds and berries are highly poisonous.

the same antiviral agent, painted on, can speed recovery.

Cold sores run in families because it is probable that the mother or father is a carrier of the virus, having already had an attack of herpes mouth ulcers some time in the past. Nothing can be done to prevent children catching the disease, but these parents must never kiss their baby's eyes for fear of infecting the eye with herpes blisters that could leave scars when healed. This rule about kissing a baby's eyes should, in fact, apply to everyone.

Q **The other day I found our four-year-old boy picking berries in the yard. He assured me he had not eaten any of them, but it has me wondering how careful we should be about potentially poisonous plants, seeds and berries.**

It is as well to regard all berries as potentially dangerous, and to take your child immediately to the hospital emergency department or your doctor if you feel that he or she has possibly been swallowing them. Be sure to take the offending berry or plant along with you for identification. But best of all, do everything you can to prevent this happening by reminding your child never to eat plants of any kind before checking with you as to what they are. Certain flowers, berries, and seeds are very attractive to children, and some— such as laburnum seeds—can be very harmful, even deadly.

Q **Could you give us an indication of when we should contact the doctor? We hate to call him unnecessarily, but are often anxious if the baby seems unwell.**

I would emphasize first that you should not be frightened to call your doctor whenever you think there is something wrong. He will be able to assess the problem and decide whether to get you to come to the office, or to go straight to the hospital. The idea that an unwell or feverish child must not be taken to see the doctor does not really make sense when you remember that he would certainly go outdoors if his illness was serious enough to require his being seen in the hospital. Obviously, in coming to a decision, the doctor will assess the risk of infection to other patients and the need to separate the child from the general waiting room.

If your doctor ever scolds you or makes you feel bad for calling him, you have the wrong doctor. This is especially the case if the ill child is a baby because babies can become desperately ill very rapidly.

Any symptom, especially in a baby, can be worrying but loss of appetite is particularly serious and usually indicates an infection. Vomiting in a baby who is not prone to vomit may also indicate the onset of infection or an obstruction. Diarrhea can be especially serious in young babies because they become dehydrated so quickly from loss of fluid. This is indicated by the symptoms of a sunken appearance of the eyes, inelastic skin, and a dry mouth.

Any change in consciousness or a convulsion is

It is never wise to delay contacting your doctor whenever you feel there is something wrong with your child. Watch particularly for symptoms of vomiting and diarrhea, which can be very serious in small babies because of the risk of dehydration.

serious, too. If your child convulses, don't panic but lay him on the bed or floor with his head to one side so that there is no risk of inhalation of vomit. Only when the convulsion has ceased should you leave him to call the doctor.

Accidents and poisoning are obvious emergencies but a difficulty arises when you are uncertain as to how harmful the substance eaten actually is. Usually it is best to go straight to the emergency room of the nearest hospital. Be sure to bring a sample of the swallowed substance with you.

It is ideal that he should vomit first but only if the poison swallowed is not a caustic or kerosene which could damage the esophagus or lungs in the process. In the United States, the Poison Control Centers are accessible to non-medical people and

you should call them to ask if you can give syrup of ipecac to make your child vomit. This, of course, requires that you have identified the poison.

Sudden difficulty in breathing is a very serious emergency indicating that something is stuck in the windpipe or in the small air tubes in the lungs. For this you must act immediately yourself (see p. 88).

In a feverish child, the actual temperature does not determine whether you should call the doctor. This is decided by your own knowledge of your child, how worried you feel and how ill he seems. A child can be very ill with a normal temperature, while in babies a subnormal level is often more serious than a rise.

Let me repeat, always contact your doctor if you are worried about your child whatever the symptom. Never be put off by the thought that he might be irritated if the condition is not serious. A good doctor wants to be contacted early in the illness.

Q **Our four-year-old son is just getting over tonsillitis. We are wondering if it is likely that his tonsils will have to be removed. How advisable is this?**

The fact that your four-year-old is just getting over an attack of tonsillitis is no reason to think he will need to have his tonsils out. It would actually be unusual for a child of his age not to have the occasional attack of tonsillitis. This especially occurs when a child starts school and comes into contact with a lot of germs from other children who have not previously been part of his environment. For the same reason, children starting school are likely to pick up a lot of colds their first year.

It is essential to be clear as to the function of the tonsils, which are the body's first line of defense for germs causing infection by air transmission when they are breathed into the body. They form part of the lymphatic system, which is a system comprising groups of lymphatic glands that are connected together by minute pipes carrying a fluid known as "lymph" that protects the body from infection. These lymphatic glands can often be felt in the neck and groin, especially in children. Their presence sometimes worries mothers who may be unaware that they are in fact normal structures.

It is important, too, to be aware that different systems of the body undergo their major growth in children at different ages. Thus development of the sexual organs takes place at puberty, around the age of eleven to fourteen. The brain grows particularly in the last half of pregnancy and the first three years of life. The growth spurt of the lymphatic system lies between these two extremes. At birth, the system is poorly developed, so that the tonsils—which are the only visible portion of the lymphatic system—can hardly be seen. By the age of between three and five years, however, they become very obvious, having grown greatly. Between eight and ten years of age, the peak of growth is reached; they then get smaller. Failure to understand that it is normal for the tonsils and adenoids—another part of the same system—to be large when the child is about four years old explains why in the past tonsils were removed unnecessarily for being "large".

The tonsils are two oval lumps on either side of the throat that can be seen when you open your mouth widely. The adenoids are similar but since they are behind the nose they cannot be seen through the mouth except with a mirror, as used by the ear, nose, and throat specialist.

Being the first line of defense, tonsils easily become inflamed and therefore greatly enlarged when undertaking their major function. Ignorance of this normal reaction led doctors in the past to recommend removal of tonsils. Yet, if someone has a boil on the hand causing it to swell, no one would recommend removal of the hand! Not so long ago, tonsils were also removed for bed-wetting and other totally disconnected problems.

Fortunately these facts are now much better understood and the widespread and needless removals of tonsils is becoming a thing of the past. Tonsils are removed for severe and recurrent tonsillitis if they have become so damaged that they no longer function. They sometimes have to be removed with the adenoids for recurrent ear infections although removal of the adenoids alone may be sufficient.

Q **Why does our five-year-old have so many nose bleeds? Is there anything we can do to prevent this?**

Nose bleeds happen more often in children, and the tendency to nose bleeds may also run in families.

The bleeding from the nose comes from the front part of the lining on the partition between the nostrils. If you look inside your child's nose, you may notice a triangular area on the partition that is more red than the rest. This is because the blood vessels or capillaries in this area are more numerous and nearer to the surface.

The area is more liable to bleed if a child injures it by picking his nose or sticking things inside the nostril.

Drying of the lining membrane also increases the chance of a nose bleed because the dried membrane can easily be damaged so that the very superficial capillaries are torn, resulting in bleeding. This particularly happens when a child has a cold that, despite the running nose, also leaves the membrane dry for part of the time.

Keeping the nostrils moist prevents bleeding. This is achieved by placing a small quantity of grease, such as vaseline, on the membrane using the little finger. A child can be taught how to do this to both sides last thing at night and first thing in the morning.

Since using this very effective method of prevention, I have not had to refer a child to an ear, nose, and throat specialist for the more traditional treatment of closing the capillaries by nasal cautery.

Q **What causes stys? This is the second one our child has had in three months. How should we treat them?**

A sty is a small boil centered on an eyelid, so that the infection lies around the root of the eyelash. In most instances, the cause is unknown but I always check for dandruff in the scalp. Where this occurs, the dandruff falls onto the eyelids so that the eyelids also contain these flakes between the eyelashes.

It is certainly always wise to keep the scalp clear of dandruff by regular shampooing. You would also be wise to extract the eyelash from the center of the sty, using fine tweezers. It does not hurt but someone will be needed to steady your child's head. This allows the pus (matter) to drain through the small hole created.

Warmth relieves the pain and encourages the pus to come out of the boil. This can be done in an old-fashioned but very effective homely way. Wrap a piece of cotton round a wooden kitchen spoon and soak it in hot water. Squeeze out the excess hot water and hold it against the sty for a few minutes.

Be sure that your child uses his own face cloth to prevent the infection from being spread to another person. Doctors sometimes prescribe an antibiotic ointment but this is really effective only if given in the early stages. When cleaning the eyes, be sure to use a separate clean piece of cotton wool for each eye.

Q **Our four-year-old seems to have very round shoulders. Can something be done to remedy this?**

You are showing an early concern about your child's round shoulders. I am quite often asked about adolescents who are round-shouldered but not four-year-olds.

I can't believe he has any disease, and therefore I find myself asking whether you are pre-set to worry about round shoulders in the way that other mothers may worry about flat feet. Did your mother keep telling *you* to stand up straight, I wonder?

Young children are so supple in their joints that I would like to to do all I can to remove your attention from his shoulders. I can think of only one rare condition that might cause the shoulders to appear round. It is associated with a short neck because of abnormal neck vertebrae and sometimes associated fixed shoulder blades. If your doctor had any suspicion that this was the cause, an X-ray would immediately give the answer.

Adolescents certainly do get round shoulders, but telling them to stand up straight only increases their self-consciousness, since the habit in girls is often an attempt to hide the emerging breasts. Sometimes the cause is that they are embarrassed by a sudden increase in height as puberty arrives. Some older children who are depressed show this in their slumping gait. Most of us walk straighter and faster when we are happy.

Most evidence suggests that special exercises do not help very much, but that is not to say that ordinary sport and every type of physical activity are not beneficial in their way.

Q **Our five-year-old seems to have flat feet. Can anything be done to improve them before they stop growing?**

I would love to know who made the diagnosis—you or your doctor. Most doctors nowadays are aware that this is an old-fashioned label. It is true that some feet look flatter than others and leave a larger mark on the floor when wet because more of the instep touches the ground. But watch what happens when he stands on tip-toe. The flat instep is pulled up into a graceful arch. The feet of babies often look flat due to a perfectly normal pad of fat in the instep. These are *fat* feet not *flat* feet.

It is the shape of the foot when on tip-toe that is important, and flat feet are so rare that such a diagnosis is seldom correct, and certainly not in children. It was frequently diagnosed in the past and exercises prescribed. But today you are much more likely to be told that your child's feet are normal.

Q **Our child seems always to breathe through his mouth rather than his nose. Could there be something wrong? What can be done to help him breathe normally?**

The first task is to check that he really is breathing through his mouth. Many doctors, as well as parents, make the mistake of believing a child is breathing through his mouth when he simply has an open mouth habit. To test whether a child is breathing through his mouth or his nostrils, take a small piece of yarn and tease out a few strands. Place these in front of his mouth and see if they are blown. The child should close his eyes. Then place some yarn

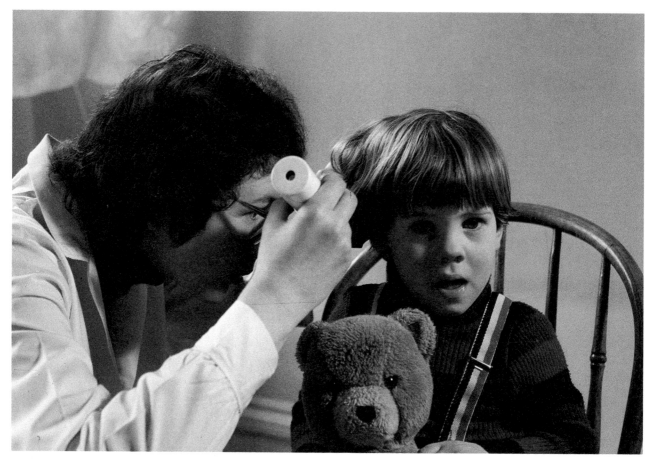

under each nostril in turn, and see if it is blown. Sometimes it may be difficult to decide whether the yarn is being moved by air coming down the nostrils or out of the mouth. In that case, place a wooden spatula (tongue depressor) or some similar object between the nose and the mouth. Some doctors use a small dental mirror or a metal tongue depressor to see in what position it becomes hazy from the exhaled air.

Far more children will be found to have an open mouth habit with a receding lower jaw than to be mouth breathers. One parent also often has a similar habit and a similarly shaped mouth, sometimes with protruding upper teeth and a receding chin.

If the child really is a mouth breather, then he may need his adenoids (not necessarily tonsils as well) removed. This is because large adenoids can block the nasal airway. This should be followed by help from a physiotherapist so that the child relearns how to breathe normally through the nose.

If he has an open mouth habit, he needs to see an orthodontist. This is a dentist who specializes in mouth shape. He will probably do nothing until the child is eight years old and his canine or eye teeth have erupted. Some orthodontists use a plastic mouth plate before this.

Once the canines are present, the orthodontists can

use wire, combined sometimes with metal frames, in order gradually to correct the position of the teeth. If there is overcrowding, he may need to remove a tooth. Treatment is continued over a period of years, but it is essential to persevere in order to improve the facial appearance, which may become embarrassing if left untreated.

Q Our three-year-old son seems to have earache very often. Why might that be? What should we do about it? Is it necessary to consult the doctor?

Earache in young children is common and must always be taken seriously since it can lead to deafness.

The ear comprises a passage leading to the tympanic membrane which is like a drum that is made to vibrate by sound waves. It forms one wall of the middle ear that contains a series of little bones (ossicles) that magnify the movements because they are arranged in the form of levers. The last lever connects with nerve fibers that lead to the inner ear and so to the brain that registers the sound.

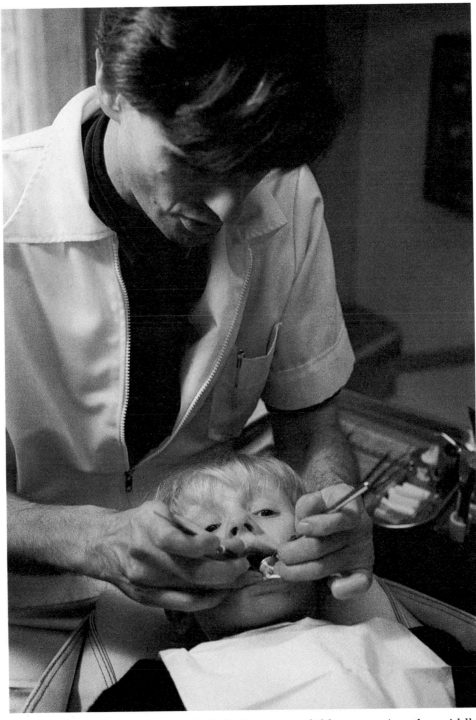

Left Fairly common in small children, earache must be taken seriously because deafness could result. It is usually due to an infection of the middle ear, but can also be caused by the insertion of a foreign body or an infection of the outer ear. Right It is important that a preventive dental program is started as early as six months when a first tooth is likely to erupt. Do everything you can both to encourage a toddler to clean his teeth and to regard the dentist as a friend.

It is important that the pressure in the middle ear, which is like a minute box, should be equal to that in the atmosphere. This is achieved by the presence of a tube leading from the back of the throat to the middle ear. It is called the eustachian tube; being an air tube, it maintains equality of air pressure between the middle ear and the outside.

The commonest cause of earache in children is infection of the middle ear. It occurs particularly in young children, causing the middle ear to be filled with a sticky glue-like material in most instances. This "glue" (giving the name "glue ear" to the condition) prevents the levers from working freely, thereby causing some pain but more importantly a degree of deafness.

Infection of the middle ear should be treated urgently. The doctor makes the diagnosis by finding the tympanic membrane fixed. When he punctures it, the middle ear is found to contain "glue." Antihistamine drops are sometimes effective in opening the eustachian tube and may first be prescribed. If this fails, the ENT (ear, nose and throat) surgeon inserts a "grommet." This is a very small plastic tube, shaped like a stud at each end, which passes through the membrane, the stud ends keeping it in position. This air tube replaces the function of the blocked eustachian tube. Once the air is freely circulating, the lining of the middle ear that has been producing the "glue" returns to normal.

The grommet needs to stay in position for six to twelve months, though the child will find his hearing returns as soon as it is in position. If it falls out within two to three months, it must be replaced, and if it has not fallen out by eighteen months, it must be removed surgically.

In previous times, infection of the middle ear produced matter or pus that often caused the membrane to rupture. This type of infection is now much less common.

Earache may also be caused by infection of the outer ear. The other cause in children is the insertion of a foreign body, such as a bead, by the child himself. The doctor must diagnose between all these conditions, but "glue ear" is the most common.

Q **How can we best prepare our child for a first visit to the dentist?**

Your question worries me, because you are talking about a child, not a baby. I always hope that the first visit to the dentist will be at the age of six months.

As far as a six-month-old baby is concerned, all you really need to do is to get him used to having fingers and a toothbrush put into his mouth. If all this is done as a game, there is usually little problem. Obviously, it is wise to get a baby used to your fingers before you start playing with any brush. Rub your finger up and down his tooth, if he has one.

Sadly, one has to accept that there will be some children of toddler age who are making their first visit to the dentist. Help your child to look on the dentist as a friend, and not someone he should fear. Tell your child that on the first occasion the dentist is likely only to have a look at his teeth. Explain that he will also probably offer a ride in his special chair which can be made to go up and down. Point out, too, that by keeping your child's teeth healthy, the dentist is going to keep them looking nice and free from pain.

I always hope, too, that the dentist will keep you in the room, since your child is much more likely to be frightened without you.

Q **How will I know if my child has measles?**

You may already have a clue to the possibility because he has been in contact with someone with measles, and therefore you are on your guard, should he be unwell. The most common first symptom is that the child is feverish and has inflammation of the eyes. There may be a fleeting rash at this time, but not the true rash of measles itself. This fleeting rash is sometimes called *prodromal*.

If you were to take your child to the doctor at this stage, he might find little white spots, termed "Koplik's spots," on the inside of the mouth that occur only early on in the disease and last for a few days. Although the Koplik's spots disappear, the lining of the inside of the cheek is left inflamed and rather rough.

About the third day, the true rash of measles appears. It starts behind the ears and then spreads to involve the face, trunk, and limbs. It covers large areas of the body in a somewhat zigzag pattern, and turns brown as the days go on. Once the rash starts to fade, peeling occurs at the site of the rash.

Although the eyes are inflamed and the child very miserable, there is no risk to the eyesight, so the old-fashioned approach of putting the child in a darkened room is totally unnecessary. It is bad enough to have measles, without being put in the dark as well.

Q **Our four-year-old is definitely overweight. Would it do any harm to put her on a diet?**

If your four-year-old is truly overweight in the sense of being considerably above the average weight, and looks fat, then it would be wrong *not* to put her on a diet.

Being fat is a considerable disadvantage to a child who is likely to be teased and will certainly win none of the races at school. Worst of all, becoming fat when young can be difficult to correct because it is possible that the child makes more fat cells that go on "asking" to be filled up.

The diet does not need to be complicated but should be based on straightforward principles. Concentrate on protein foods such as fish, meat, cheese, and eggs. Reduce her fat and carbohydrate intake by cutting down on bread, cakes, and butter as much as possible. And cut out desserts. It will not be too awful at first for the child as long as there are no sweets or chocolate in the house. This will not do you any harm either! Remember that milk is fattening, too.

To fill the gap in her hunger, you can give her as much salad and other green foods as she will take. The trouble is that she may not like them, though once she realizes there are no alternatives, she may change her mind.

Keep a weight chart and make her proud of losing weight. Prizes are in order, if they are toys or cash for toys, and not food. If, like some parents, you fear putting a child on a diet although you know that many adults have to diet, turn your fear the other way around so that you are frightened of *obesity*. Make sure, too, that grandparents understand the seriousness of being too fat, so they do not allow their natural sympathy to lead to the giving of candy on the sly.

Lastly, make sure the school knows what is going on and plays its part. School lunches could undo all the good that goes on at home, if you aren't careful. Fortunately, however, most school meals are now far less stodgy and children aren't made to "eat up."

Q **Why does our four-year-old son so often get "a stitch" when he runs? What is it that causes the sudden pain in his side?**

It would be interesting to know the cause of a "stitch" but I have never heard of a satisfactory physiological explanation. I am very aware that some children develop pain in the side of the abdomen when running, and I recollect having this pain myself. But I do not remember ever hearing from an adult who has had the symptom.

I suspect it is due to intestinal distention resulting from a collection of gas in one loop of the intestine. Rest and bending towards the pain is usually successful in getting rid of it. I have never known a child come to harm from a stitch, though I am under no illusion that it can cause considerable discomfort so that it may stop a child from being able to run for a short time.

Q **Can you explain what causes ringworm and how we should treat it? How could our four-year-old daughter have caught it?**

Ringworm is due to a fungus (not a worm despite its name) that is only visible under the microscope. There are a number of varieties that affect different parts of the body. The most common sites in children are the scalp and the skin on the trunk and limbs. In ringworm of the scalp, the hair breaks and comes out, leaving one or more bald patches. When ringworm occurs on the skin, the patches are circular in shape and gradually grow outwards, while healing in the center.

Ringworm is caught from someone else with the same infection, or from animals, especially cats. Ringworm of the scalp is particularly infectious, so children are kept from school until cured. Fortunately, today this takes only about three weeks because a new and very effective antidote has been discovered. A child with ringworm must keep to his own towels, brushes, combs, and clothes.

Q **Would you recommend that we give routine multi-vitamin supplements to our four-year-old son? He is rather picky about his food and rarely finishes a meal. We are concerned that he is not eating enough.**

Your reference to your four-year-old being picky about his food suggests to me that you are more concerned about his eating than most parents. I think this way because children whose parents are totally unconcerned about how much they eat usually eat like horses!

Children are so sensitive to those areas of behavior about which their parents are concerned that they play up in almost standard ways. Food concern often leads to picking at meals and even to food refusal. Similarly bowel concern may lead to stool-holding and soiling.

Everyone has his brain "computer" set by his parents' methods of handling him when young. I am therefore bound to wonder whether there was concern that *you* should "eat up" when *you* were very young.

If my deductions are correct, your question about vitamin supplements follows a concern that, because he does not eat as much as you would like him to, you feel he should have extra vitamins just in case he goes short. You have to be grossly starved to go short of vitamins, and it is not a problem I meet among children in this country. If a child is energetic, he is getting enough food.

My advice, therefore, is to forget about vitamins unless, of course, he shows some clinical evidence of vitamin deficiency which I cannot believe to be the case. Stop showing any interest in what he eats or what he doesn't eat. Choose the foods he likes, even if he keeps wanting the same thing—children are very conservative people. Never say "eat up." Give him small helpings. He can ask for more if he wants, and remove his plate at the end of the meal whether or not it is empty.

Provide your child with meat, fish, eggs and cheese for protein, fresh fruit and vegetables, and not too much carbohydrate in the form of potatoes, bread and cakes, and the chances are that he or she will be getting a very well balanced diet. Vitamin supplements are rarely necessary.

Remember that children are rather conservative about their food: so you may find you have to serve the foods they like rather than varying the menu greatly. In general, where parents appear unconcerned about "eating up", there are few appetite problems.

The worst possible thing is to make a child sit over his uneaten food. This is pure torture, and the amazing thing is the frequency with which parents, who had the same treatment meted out to them and hated it, behave in the same way towards their own children. You will find that once you take the pressure off, he will begin to eat much more.

Q **When should we start to look after our child's teeth in order to ensure that they are healthy? Is a fluoride toothpaste advisable?**

This is all part of the preventive dental program that I hope all infants will receive.

The dental hygienist will advise whether it is a good idea for your toddler to be given fluoride either as drops or tablets, since this may form an important part of the preventive dental program in areas where the level of fluoride in the water is low. Check that your child knows how to clean his teeth correctly: and perhaps try using disclosure tablets to show him just how vigorously he needs to brush in order to remove any plaque.

If the child enters the program at the age of six months, he or she should emerge at the age of sixteen with a set of perfectly healthy teeth.

The most important person in this program is the dental hygienist. He or she has been trained to protect the teeth from decay. Starting at six months, which is when the first tooth erupts on the average, the hygienist will show you how to use fluoride. This is on the assumption that you are in an area where the fluoride level is low. (You can check this with your dentist or water board.) The fluoride is given initially as drops, but later as tablets. It is also contained in many toothpastes.

The dental hygienist will advise you about the cleaning of your baby's teeth, and particularly the right type of toothbrush. This should be short and with soft bristles. The old idea of tough bristles was quite wrong. You should clean the teeth with an up-and-down movement as this is much more effective and does not harm the gums.

An additional method of removing material lying between the teeth is the use of floss. This is a strong but fine thread which you insert between the teeth.

The dental hygienist will also be watching for any cracks or fissures in the teeth that need to be sealed.

All these methods prevent the formation of plaque which leads to dental decay. The hygienist will check, too, on the alignment of the teeth as they erupt. If the teeth are overcrowded, it might be necessary to call in the help of the orthodontist who is a specialist with the role of ensuring straight teeth.

For the older child who is reluctant to clean his teeth, you might try using disclosure tablets. These are sucked by the child, and leave a brightly colored staining where there is plaque, which can then be removed with vigorous brushing. This gives a good indication of just how much brushing is required. Children usually find the tablets fun to use as, more often than not—since they may not have been brushing properly—they will end up with their teeth stained bright red or blue!

Q **Why might our three-year-old be constipated so often? What should we do to prevent constipation? How concerned should we be about it? Could it be due to diet?**

The first question I would like to ask is what you mean by "constipation." Constipation means so many different things to different people. Working in Africa, I even found that some mothers were describing diarrhea, though using the word constipation!

My next question would be what is it that worries you about the symptom because I would be very doubtful if your child's health is being affected. In order to work out the problem, I would need a detailed history. Aspects such as your approach to training and how *you* were handled when young are all of relevance.

There is a common belief that failure to have a daily motion can be dangerous to health. Your question refers to frequent constipation, so clearly you are not discussing acute intestinal obstruction, nor do you refer to any evidence of illness.

I would be particularly interested to know your parents' attitude to your bowels when young because that is the time the pattern is so often set for how parents handle their own children later. It was not uncommon in the last century for babies to be sat on potties on their mothers' knees from birth. This set up a conditioned reflex so that the baby's bowels opened when the rim of the pot touched the skin of the buttocks. But this reflex lasts a few months only, so that it was not long before the child reacted against the reflex and held back the stools.

This was commonly misunderstood by the parents, since the child appeared to be straining to open the bowels when in reality the action was to prevent such opening. The answer lies in checking on the child's position. If the legs are crossed, he is trying to hold back the stool whereas a child straining to open his bowels assumes a squatting position.

Children commonly become miserable for the few days before the strength of the bowel waves (peristalsis) overcomes their ability to hold back the stools. Such behavior is commonly misinterpreted as straining to open when it is actually straining to hold back. Such "stool-holders" can feel great distress at the loss of the stool, brought about by acquired negativistic behavior as a reaction to parental misunderstanding.

Babies are not the only ones to react to parental bowel pressures. Vets tell me that puppies brought up in such a household may even eat the stool to avoid punishment for being discovered doing it in the wrong place.

The one essential is to adopt an attitude of total nonconcern about the child's bowels. Laxatives, suppositories, and enemas only increase the child's negativistic reaction. No healthy child comes to any harm from not having the bowels open every day, though associated soiling in the acute phase is common. On no account must the child be punished.

I never prescribe a special diet for children, like fiber, and don't believe exercise makes any difference. This is a behavior problem, not a food one. A child may even go two to three weeks between bowel actions and come to no harm. Such a child is likely to soil himself but still he must not be punished.

Q **I would like to know what to do as an emergency procedure should our child ever choke on a bone or a piece of candy. What is the best thing to do if this happens? What is the immediate action to take?**

The first and immediate action is to look inside the mouth in the hope that you can see and remove the object, using tweezers for a bone. If this fails, the standard emergency measure for years has been to hold the child upside down and bang his back. However, there is now a fear that this could cause the object to be drawn further down into the lungs. For this reason, a new method, termed the Heimlich maneuvre, has been invented.

The aim here is to blow out the object by the force of air produced by the technique. The child is held upright with the adult standing behind. A fist is made with your clasped hands, and these are then jerked backwards towards the spine, causing the air to be forced out of the lungs.

Obviously, young children should never be left eating on their own, and on no account should dangerous objects, like candy, be within the grasp of a baby. I would hope that foods containing bones would never be given. The most dangerous object is a peanut because it contains an oil that causes the lining of the air tube to swell. Consequently, the air tube blocks long before this would occur with a nonirritating substance.

The damaged lining can cause permanent harm because the part of the lung further on is drained of air and may never re-expand. The golden rule is no peanuts in the house before the age of about eight years. Worst of all, and of greatest danger, is a child's habit of throwing up peanuts and catching them in his mouth.

Q How might our toddler have caught athlete's foot? How is it best treated? Can it be prevented?

I am very surprised that someone as young as a toddler should catch athlete's foot because it is a problem that particularly affects school children and adults. The disease is caused by ringworm, which is a fungus and is highly infectious, spreading by contact, especially in bathing areas.

Numerous skin applications are available. These are being constantly improved and your doctor will prescribe what he feels is best for your child. Meticulous attention must be paid to washing and drying of the feet.

Encourage your child to wear sandals and to do without socks whenever possible because heat encourages the growth of the fungus.

Q Our four-year-old is badly asthmatic. What is the best way for us to handle an attack?

Prevention is the essential approach. This means avoiding anything that brings on an attack. Many children are sensitive to the microscopic mite that lives on shed skin in house dust. Therefore you must do everything to keep the dust down. Dust with a damp cloth, vacuum-clean the upholstery, especially in the crevices of the chairs, and change the bedding often. Shake the blankets, but only when your child is out of the room and out of the house if possible.

Physiotherapy should be taught as a way of life to to all those who get asthma. This means that parents should learn breathing and postural exercises to undertake with the child, as well as percussion and postural drainage (tipping and thumping) for use in an attack as soon as your child will let you. By this means, you can clear the accumulation of phlegm and hasten the end of the attack.

Running tends to precipitate wheezing but swimming does not. All asthmatic children should swim as much as possible. Emotional factors often play a part, and so it is important to do what you can to keep your child on an even keel—not always easy.

There are two sorts of drugs that are applicable: those that are given all the time to prevent attacks and those that are used during an attack, preferably as early as possible. These may be given by mouth or intravenously, or you may be provided with a special aerosol inhaler that can be very effective. I am not going to list the

names of the drugs because that is your own doctor's responsibility, but the good thing is that we now have much more effective medicines for asthma than in the past but they must be given early in an attack. If you know or sense the attack is a dangerous one, you must rush your child to a hospital, but start the home treatment *before* setting off on the journey.

Be sure to learn all about the medicines. It is important that you are clear which are for preventing attacks and therefore given daily, irrespective of attacks, and which are for use the moment an attack starts.

Try to work out and reduce the emotional factors and be sure to keep calm when he has an attack because fear is so catching.

Q What exactly is cystic fibrosis? What causes it? Is it a life-long condition?

Cystic fibrosis (CF) is an inherited condition that is fortunately rare although it has been the subject of much publicity. The disorder was first described in 1938. It particularly affects the pancreas gland in the abdomen, which produces digestive enzymes, and also the lungs.

Failure of digestion causes the child to grow less well than normal and therefore to be thin and shorter than average. The abdomen sticks out and the stools, which are bulky and pale, have a very offensive odor.

Involvement of the lungs causes repeated chest infections and this is the most serious part of the illness. In fact, the health of an individual child with CF and his life expectancy are determined by whether or not the lungs are involved and, if so, how severely.

The age at which the diagnosis is made depends on the relative involvement of the pancreas and the lungs. The child fails to thrive and is liable to have repeated chest infections. But the good news is that not all children are severely affected. Moreover, most can lead a normal life between bouts of infection and very few require special schooling. I have been looking after a patient from birth who is now a well-built man of twenty who has never suffered from lung infections. His problems have been digestive.

The cause of CF is still not fully known. The mucus produced in the body is very sticky but exactly why this is so is not understood. Modern treatment with antibiotics and pancreatic enzymes has made a great difference to the future of affected children. The Cystic Fibrosis Foundation has given support to families in every possible way, as well as very actively supporting research into the disorder.

It is principally a concern about obesity and its associated problems that has led to widespread publicity about the risks of drinking too much milk. A pint of milk each day could be too much for your child.

Right Immunization schedules vary from country to country, but in general protection will be given against diphtheria, whooping cough and tetanus, as well as polio, during the first few months on three separate occasions. In the United States, immunization against measles and also mumps will follow, and later against tuberculosis and German measles (rubella).

Parents should always be told that it is inherited and that both of them must be carriers even though they do not have the disease. Research continues in an attempt to find a method for detecting carriers. The risk that future children will be affected is in the ratio of one to four, but it must be emphasized that this is a population figure and not a family figure. On this basis, two out of four will be carriers and one will be normal. This is the normal "recessive" rate of inheritance.

 Our three-year-old seems to have knock knees. Should we consult a pediatrician? Is it something to be concerned about?

If a child has knock knees, the legs below the knees turn outwards when the sides of the knees are touching. This causes the ankles to become separated. A mild degree of knock knees is normal between the ages of three and seven years. This

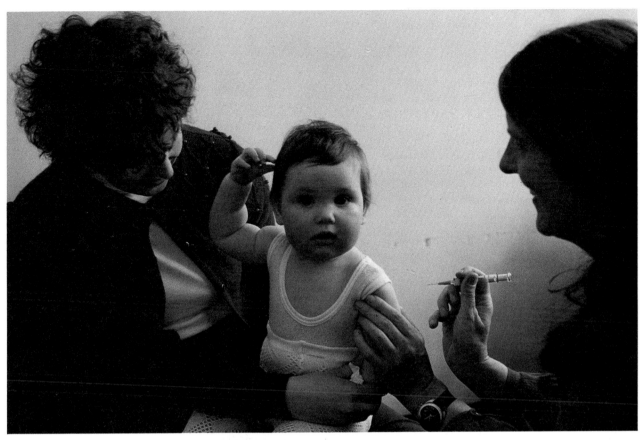

gradually corrects itself without treatment as a consequence of normal growth. In the past, shoes were altered by building up the inner edge of the sole, but this is no longer felt to be necessary.

To test for knock knees, put your fingers between your child's ankles when he is lying on his back with his knees pointing directly at the ceiling. Normally, you can place two fingers, side by side, between the ankles; more than this indicates abnormal knock knees. The cause of an abnormal degree of knock knees is excessive weight. Consequently you need do nothing if testing shows the amount of knock knees to be within normal limits, but if it is more than this, he is almost certainly overweight and needs dieting. Splints, manipulations, and ultraviolet light are old fashioned and have no place in modern treatment.

important cause of obesity. In days gone by, though sadly still very much so in developing countries, extra milk was an easy source of extra calories. But obesity is actually the main variety of malnutrition in Great Britain today. I would like to see a pint of milk being given to selected children from poor homes. Certainly, it should not be given as a routine to all children, many of whom are too fat, so that it could be too much for your child.

Fat babies used to be called bonny, presumably from the French work "bon" meaning good. I suspect they were "good" because they were stupefied by so much food. Today, however, we realize that obesity increases the risk of diseases of the heart and blood vessels and shortens life expectancy.

Q I have noticed that there has been a lot of publicity lately about the dangers of drinking too much milk. Is a pint of milk a day too much for our five-year-old?

The main reason for this publicity is the relatively recent concern about overweight. Milk has a high fat content and is therefore an

Q Immunization seems so complicated to understand. What should our baby have, and when?

Fortunately, it is not as complicated as it sounds. You will also have lots of people to help you, particularly your family doctor, pediatrician, or public health services. They will probably give you a booklet that shows which shots your baby should have and when. As each shot is given, a record is made in the booklet so that you know exactly where you are.

Immunization schedules vary somewhat from country to country. In the United States, the first immunization is a combination of diphtheria, whooping cough, and tetanus, given as an injection. It is called DPT, since whooping cough is also known as *pertussis*. On the same occasion, the baby is given polio vaccine as a liquid by mouth, using a dropper— or, in older children, on a lump of sugar. In the United States, the recommended ages for this combination of DPT and polio are two months, four months, and six months. A booster dose of DPT and polio is given at eighteen months and again when the child is four– six years of age.

In the United States, immunization is given against mumps together with German measles (*rubella*) and measles. One dose against all three diseases is given at fifteen months. Although *rubella* is a mild illness, the reason for trying to eradicate the disease is that an attack in pregnancy can cause abnormalities of the growing fetus.

BCG vaccination protects against tuberculosis and is named after its three discoverers. The policy varies in different countries. In the United States, tuberculosis testing is routinely undertaken at twelve months of age. The majority of babies are negative and no further step is taken. Only if there is a later possibility of contact with a patient with tuberculosis is the child re-tested.

Q **I keep hearing about the importance of immunization against German measles. Can you tell me something about this? At what age is it usually given?**

I am very glad that you do keep hearing about immunization against German measles, and I hope that, as a woman, you have been immunized yourself. The reason for this is that German measles, which is due to a virus, can cause abnormalities of the fetus if the adult who gets it is a pregnant woman. The risk is greatest early in pregnancy, while the vital organs are being formed. This is why girls at school, between the ages of eleven and fourteen, are offered German measles vaccination. Be sure to accept this for your daughter when the time comes. In some countries, including the United States, boys are also offered the vaccination.

Some girls unfortunately miss their vaccination at the proper age. They must ensure that they are vaccinated against German measles, but must also ensure they do not become pregnant for three months from the date of the vaccination. The

reason for this is that the virus in the vaccine, while causing no harm to the adult, might damage the fetus.

Q **Would you recommend that we consider immunization against whooping cough for our baby?**

I would very definitely recommend immunization against whooping cough or *pertussis*, as it is also known, as long as none of the recognized contraindications exist. Whooping cough can be very serious, particularly in babies. It causes a long, drawn-out illness that is extremely distressing both to the infant and to his parents. The cough may continue for weeks, and it can damage the lungs.

Babies are especially upset because they do not acquire the knack of whooping, whereby the breath is taken in very rapidly at the end of a bout of coughing, causing the characteristic whoop. Vomiting is common, and the child is not only seriously ill but is also likely to lose a considerable amount of weight and to pick up other illnesses.

Immunization against whooping cough has greatly reduced the number of cases and, although some immunized children catch the disease, it is less serious than it would otherwise have been.

Like most parents, probably the principal reason you are asking this question about whooping cough immunization is the fear that has been created by the very rare complication of inflammation of the brain following immunization. This has been grossly exaggerated, and the risk is much less than the risk of serious harm from the illness. It has in fact been discovered by means of electrical tests of the brain that whooping cough itself has an effect on the brain, even when none is obvious.

The greatest argument in favor of immunization is the tremendous drop in the number of cases since it became available. It is probable that additional factors, such as improved living conditions, have also influenced this, but there is no doubt that immunization is the main reason.

The doctor undertaking the immunization should always check for contraindications. These include brain symptoms at birth suggesting lack of oxygen; a history of convulsions—in the child or in a close relation; or a serious reaction such as continuous crying after a previous immunization shot for whooping cough. Lastly, the child must be well when given the shot. It should be postponed if he has a cold.

The wisdom of having your child immunized is best shown by the recent epidemics of whooping cough in Great Britain that have resulted from the drop in the immunization level in that country following the scare about brain damage.

Q **My little boy has mumps. I have heard it may prevent him from having children. Is that really so? How dangerous is this disease?**

Fortunately, this is very unlikely to occur to your son. This is because you are referring to a young child, whereas the risk of damage to the testicles is in adolescents and adults who catch mumps. Mumps seldom attacks both testicles anyway. Therefore, the number of men who have been made sterile as a result of mumps is very small.

Q **Our two-year-old son has eczema. What causes it? Will he grow out of it, and what is the best way to manage the condition? Is there any cure?**

Eczema is one of the allergic diseases, and its presence indicates that your child is sensitive to a protein substance that does not affect other children. Many aspects of the disorder are unknown, including details of the cause, but it is the child's immune system that is not working to his benefit. In a sense, in fact, it is over-reacting.

Eczema seldom appears before the age of two to three months, so that spots in newborn babies that are common are not due to this cause. It is not unusual for children with eczema to suffer from asthma, too, and for some reason that has not been explained, the condition tends to fluctuate in severity in a seesaw fashion. The substance causing eczema is something that comes in contact with the skin. Nurses sometimes become allergic to antibiotic powders so gloves are worn to prevent unnecessary contact. Those children who develop asthma have been born with an unduly sensitive lining to the air tubes, comparable to the similar extra sensitivity that occurs in the lining of the nose in those with hay fever.

There is a tendency to improve with age, and usually it is in the early months that the condition is at its most severe. When older, many children get eczema only in the fronts of the elbows and the backs of the knees.

The best way to manage the condition is very clear-cut, namely, to work out which substance is causing the eczema and to avoid all contact. Obviously, this is not always possible, though an experimental period of trial and error using bland substances for washing may be remarkably successful. Potentially irritating substances, such as detergents, must be avoided when washing clothes. Many children with eczema have greasy hair and dandruff. This must be eradicated, and your doctor will help.

A child is either born with a tendency to eczema or not. Since there is no complete cure, your child must avoid those substances that, when applied to the skin, bring on the condition. Your doctor will also be able to supply ointments that protect the skin. Cortisone is often successful, but since it is a strong application, I prefer tar ointment for routine use, keeping cortisone in reserve. Many mothers fear cortisone and consequently use very little when more is actually required. On the other hand, tar ointment—though messy—is remarkably effective and the child can be given his own jar, if old enough, and can apply as much as he wants. Despite the mess it makes, tar is an old-fashioned but very effective application.

A special soapy emulsifying ointment is used instead of soap because it is nonirritant. This can be smeared over the baby before putting him in the bath, but beware of the slipperiness once it has been applied. The alternative is to put the ointment in the bath before the baby and to stir it up.

The possibility that breastfeeding protects from eczema has been raised. The evidence for this is not definite, but it is ideal that babies should be breastfed in any case.

Q **I have heard it said that peanuts can be dangerous to children? Why should this be so?**

It is absolutely true, and I only wish that all parents knew of this very considerable danger. The problem is that the child may inhale the peanut instead of swallowing it, so that it goes down into his lungs instead of into his stomach. This risk, of course, is made greater by the habit that many children have of throwing the peanut up in the air and catching it in the mouth.

Peanuts are a much greater hazard than any other foreign body because they not only block the small air tube but the oil they contain causes an acute inflammation of the lining of the air tube. Permanent damage may result.

Because of these dangers, it should be a rule that no child under the age of eight is allowed peanuts.

Index